Principles
of Canoeing

THE MACMILLAN COMPANY
NEW YORK • CHICAGO
DALLAS • ATLANTA • SAN FRANCISCO
LONDON • MANILA

THE MACMILLAN COMPANY
OF CANADA, LIMITED
TORONTO

Principles of Canoeing

PIERRE PULLING

(Albert Van Siclen Pulling)

Drawings by
NELLIE C. JARVIS

New York 1954

THE MACMILLAN COMPANY

*To the Canadian Bush
and the Canadian Voyageur*

Author's Preface

A preface is sometimes arid reading. But before you skip this one, I implore a little patience while I explain how this book is planned, and why.

The Principles of Canoeing has been arranged in such a way that each chapter is a more or less separate unit. In achieving this a little repetition has been unavoidable. I have tried to be brief. But I have indulged in a few personal anecdotes here and there, in order to nail down—I hope!—important points.

This book is for everyone interested in canoes and canoeing. If you have little or no experience in the art, and have no part in an organized program of instruction, you will find the earlier chapters of greatest value, but you may take helpful hints from all of them. If you are a hunter or fisherman, you will probably read Chapter 9 first—it is written especially for you—and then refer to others for such additional information as you may need.

But camp, school, or club canoeing instructors will do well to grind through everything. Canoe experts—and there are many—will find the book most useful as a reference text. And specialists will of course be interested in reading anything and everything on canoeing. I am.

Every writer on a special subject has his own view-point. Mine is primarily that of the Canadian woods professional and guide. I learned canoeing because I had to in order to do my work; and I still regard the canoe chiefly as a vehicle for getting around in waters in which it is the best or only suitable means of transportation. I coached camp canoeists for a dozen years, and acted as a camp consultant for many more; but I did it with canoe travel as my chief objective. I have raced too, and coached racers—largely using woods canoes for the purpose, just as range riders race with cow ponies and stock saddles.

Out of this practical experience I have developed ideas about some points in canoeing—especially methods of paddling and names for paddle strokes—that are at variance with the practices and written instructions of some of the major canoeing groups. Thirty-odd years ago, about the time that I was assisting the opposition to the late Kaiser Wilhelm II, there arose a school of thought which held that, in paddling, both arms should be held as stiff and straight as pokers at all times. This method has now been largely abandoned by canoeing teachers; but at one time it was all the rage, and it still has backers here and there. It has always seemed to me to be awkward, unnatural, and inefficient.

At approximately the same time, many groups and teachers became interested in an exhaustive study of paddle strokes. Now the basic strokes are few and easy; but varying conditions of wind, water, and load —not to mention paddle length, canoe size, and the paddler's physique—may cause them to be used in an almost endless series of variations and combinations. You could, if you tried, analyze dozens of different "strokes," and give names to them all. Nobody to my knowledge has gone to such lengths, but in the 1920's things were tending in that direction. What's more, different groups were using different names for the same stroke, and there was consequently a good deal of confusion. The result was that, in 1930, a poll was taken among the major organizations concerned with canoeing nomenclature, and at that time the stroke names in current use were adopted. They are now official with the five principal groups—the American Camping Association, the American Red Cross, the Boy Scouts, the Girl Scouts, and the Camp Fire Girls. I have referred to these names, and to the strokes which they designate, later in this book. They are commonly used by canoeing instructors in the vast majority of summer camps.

But in my own coaching I have come to believe that the accepted names are for the most part inaccurate and unduly complicated. They seemed to hold up the progress of learners rather than to help it. So I have developed my own stroke names—fewer and simpler than those on the approved list—and those are the ones I have used in Chapter 4 of this book. My names may not be the best that could be devised, but they are more descriptive, more accurate, and easier to use in teaching than the dozen or so approved in 1930.

In this, as in the entire book, I have tried to present canoeing as the simple and beautiful art that it is. So I have included little about war canoes or canoe racing, which are relatively minor specialties; and nothing at all on "formal" canoeing, which has virtually died out. Nor have I stressed canoe trips, as they are largely canoeing plus camping—and camping is the subject of my *next* book, not the present one. But I have covered the fundamentals as clearly and accurately as I could—the things that should be known by everyone who ventures into a canoe, whether for an hour's drifting among the lily pads in a summer twilight, or a month-long canoe-and-portage trip through a chain of wilderness lakes and wild, white-water streams.

In its essentials, *Principles of Canoeing* is a natural outgrowth of my earlier book, *Elements of Canoeing*, which was published in 1933 and has long been out of print. With the exception of certain quotations and an occasional sentence, it has been completely rewritten, and one chapter is entirely new.

All the persons and organizations who helped with the earlier book were of course most valuable in developing this one. And I must give thanks to many others, several of whom were indispensable.

Perhaps J. R. T. Bueno and Macmillan's Carol H. Woodward should be mentioned first, for their patient editorial assistance; and immediately after them Nellie Jarvis, who typed all the manuscript and made many drawings. The contributions of Ann Elizabeth Weber and W. Van B. Claussen have been immeasurably great. Emily Welch of the American Camping Association, a friend since 1925, has assisted Miss Woodward and me with her good advice. Nearly all the canoe manufacturers of both Canada and the United States gave me useful information, and I received invaluable data from the Canadian Canoe Company of Peterborough, Ontario; the E. M. White Canoe Company of Old Town, Maine; and the Grumman Aircraft Engineering Corporation of Bethpage, Long Island, New York. For the freest use of the facilities at Idaho State College while I was preparing the text, I am especially indebted to President Carl W. McIntosh; to John Vesser, Director of Athletics; to Byrne Fernelius, swimming coach; and to Chester Cooper, film librarian.

For several fine photographs I am grateful to Donald Pugmire, and for their assistance to Idaho State College students Patricia Lavens Jones, Sally Ann Bennett, Niobe Larsen and Arlene Jones, as well as the basketball coach Steve Belko. Photographers Dale Carringer, Rufus Lyman, and Walter Merryman also made valuable contributions; while the W. A. Fisher Company of Virginia, Minnesota, and Canoe Country Outfitters of Ely, Minnesota, likewise furnished excellent cooperation.

There is another group that I must also mention. This is the professional guides and woodsmen of

Canada, dozens of whom contributed to my canoeing education by precept and example. The most important of them were Isadore Meconse, an Abnaki Indian of Mont Laurier, Quebec, with whom I worked in 1914, and a Huron known only as Eugene, with whom I paddled in 1916 at the Triton Club in Quebec. Guides Charles Cremin and Victor Moore gave me my first really good poling information on the Tobique River in New Brunswick in 1920. Guides Jack Legault of the Algoma District of Ontario, with whom I worked in 1930–33, and Lloyd Melville, with whom I took a long trip on the east coast of Hudson's Bay in 1937, were both heavy contributors to such professional canoeing knowledge as I possess. Their endorsement was responsible for my membership in the Algoma Guides Association.

Roman numerals in the text refer to the bibliography, which follows the Appendix. I have tried to make it inclusive, listing everything of interest to American canoeists and much of use to American oarsmen. While it is up to date, including both new publications and the latest revisions of older ones, it also contains some books known to be out of print and some magazines known to be discontinued. These are marked with an asterisk (*), and are listed for their historical interest and as research aids to investigators. It is but fair to add that not all the works named are, in my opinion, equally valuable. They vary from the reasonably sublime to the—well, considerably less so. But attempting to separate the sheep from the goats is a thankless task; nor can I question that what is meat for one reader may be poison for another.

Following the bibliography is a list of all the factory-size canoe makers of which I know in the United States and Canada. A considerable number of these also make paddles and other canoe and boat equipment.

PIERRE PULLING

Idaho State College
Pocatello, Idaho
June, 1954

Contents

List of Figures

Introduction

The canoe is the most interesting link that unites the past and the future. It may be the only still popular but truly aboriginal tool that we have inherited. Its beauty and grace continue to intrigue the artist, yet it carries its master and his property with a competent mulish buoyancy.

The changeless pack or saddle animal is the only transportation device that I can compare with the canoe. Trade, romance, religion, adventure, and erudition all halo faithful beasts of burden and equally faithful canoes. A faithful donkey carried the young Christ into Egypt. Smashing ancestors of the Clydesdale bore knights into battle. Sleek Arabians made up Coronado's cavalry. Canoes, however, transported Jesuit missionaries to the four winds of eastern America. Canoes carried much of the local freight of an early civilization. Canoes sailed unbelievable distances in the South Seas. Canoes, in gondola form, are still the most romantic craft in the world's most artistic country.

As other early tools give ground, the canoe and a few of its associates increase in popularity. It is still the willing slave of the prospector, the hunter, the fisherman, the camper, and the adventurer. The hunter may pursue game or romance. The angler may be a fisher of salmon or of men. The prospector can be seeking gold or art. The paddling camper is often escaping from civilization's boredom, while the canoeing adventurer is re-living the days of the Fur Brigade over the largely unchanged waters of Canada.

1.   Running fast water in a canoe.

Like the pack-string, the canoe is as old as history and as young as tomorrow's sunrise. Its future is as certain as its present. The best canoes ever built are on the modern market, and nothing of such beauty, grace, and utility can ever grow old.

Still, as in the days of yore, the canoe demands a master. I repeat that it is mulish. Some say "cranky." A horse or a dog may work through sheer devotion to any human, but a mule's handler must know more than a mule. A clumsy barge may slowly and safely transport gross baggage with a crude pilot. The canoe is docile only when managed with skill and judgment. Nothing inanimate is so human, though the small sailboat, including the sailing canoe, is comparable. One cannot, like Hiawatha, guide his canoe solely by thought, but the elements of paddling are so simple that thought becomes action with no apparent time lapse.

Complementary to the modern charm and fascinating background of the canoe is the fact that master canoeists are still around. Like master mariners in sail, they are rarer than they were, but canoeing is no lost art. There are canoeists both at home and abroad who can do anything with a canoe that anyone ever did. Furthermore, they can teach almost anyone excellent canoeing.

Though no older art is quite comparable to canoeing, excellent bows, Kentucky-type rifles, fine saddlery, and the best axes of all time are available today, as well as canoes and paddles. And there are still masters in the uses of all these old implements to tutor those who care.

I repeat that many of these time-honored arts are not lost. No more lost than the study of classical cultures. But now you may be fairly well educated without majoring in ancient Greek. You can cook lunch without first splitting kindling. And you may (sometimes) travel by other means on waters that once demanded a canoe. In many instances the canoe is still the most beautiful, the most logical, and the most efficient means of travel. At times it is still the only suitable craft for certain waters.

So let's stop explaining and philosophizing, and have at it!

1

Canoeing Here and There

Modern canoes are the handiest, most versatile small boats that have ever been made. For their size, they are the safest existing boats; and for their weight, they have greater carrying capacity than anything else that floats, with the possible exception of collapsible (but easily puncturable) rubber boats and rafts.

Though canoes are made primarily to be paddled, they can be rigged for sailing as easily as any other small boats, and if equipped with either a motor bracket or a square stern, a canoe that is built for working can be operated with an outboard motor. Canadian freight canoes are suitable for even inboard motors.

For years, in the Canadian woods, there was never any question as to what kind of small boat you would use. The only question was, "What kind of canoe?" The answer depended on what you meant to do.

For bush travel I have used everything from a 14-foot, 39-pound cedar-and-birch-bark job to a 22-foot, 60-inch-beam freighter that was loaded with

5,000 pounds. (Yes, two and a half *tons*. And old-time freighters, as will be noted in Chapter 2, some-times had twice the capacity of any now made.) In organized camps I have been responsible for fleets of as many as 32 canoes, varying in size from 14-foot racers to 35-foot war canoes which could carry 20 light paddlers or 12 big men.

Today, canoes are put to all sorts of uses. They turn up as Olympic Games racing craft, and as Hudson's Bay Company schooner-tenders and lifeboats. I have seen Crees and Eskimos travel 400 miles in them just to trade. I saw two young couples canoe-sail over a hundred miles to be married by the Church.

Most fresh-water fishing boats should be canoes. Nearly all hunting boats, and especially duck boats, should be canoes. Propelling hunting boats by any except hand methods is legally prohibited in this coun-try, and here is where the skilled paddler really comes into his own.

Within certain limits, the size of the water is not important. I have paddled extensively on Lake Supe-rior, Hudson's Bay, and the Missisippi River. Smaller waters fit the canoe better, but one uses what one has. Bering Strait Eskimos did all right canoeing back and forth to Siberia until the Iron Curtain was rung down.

Canoes *are* popular, and should be more popular. Some people are afraid of them, and it is true that you can upset a canoe if you don't respect its center of gravity. It is also true that many dangerously light canoes have been made, and many people have taken risks because they were not trained. It is no more safe for an untaught person to go out in a canoe than for an untaught motorist to drive in Chicago traffic the first time he touches a steering wheel. I have, however, seen people with no training whatever go into dangerous water in a canoe, in the hope that they could swim out of an accident.

I repeat that a canoe is the world's safest boat for its size. This assumes that it is handled with propriety and judgment. It is used in that very dangerous element, water. In a sense any boat is dangerous, just as any loaded gun is dangerous, or any car with gasoline in it. In the last analysis, however, it is the canoeists, the gun handlers, and the drivers who are dangerous. Many people are hurt and some are killed by slipping in bathtubs! Yet the bathtub is not blamed for human carelessness.

As the reader masters this little book, these facts should become very apparent. I am not sure that studying a book can make you a canoeist any more than book work will make you a rifleman, a horseman, or a truck driver. Books on these arts are valuable, however, and so is a book on canoeing.

Please note that anyone, or almost anyone, can learn to handle a canoe. If you can play golf—or even bridge—you can paddle. I have taught paddlers with no prevous training from the ages of six to more than sixty, and among many hundreds I have personally handled, I recall only two who were utter failures. These two were apparently so badly coordinated that they could not learn anything demanding a little physical skill.

Like horses, dogs, bows, and axes, canoes are, in a sense, relics of the past. Even so, there are more canoes in use right now in this country than ever before. The K-9 Corps, the military carrier pigeon, and the special deer seasons for archers all point to a revival of ancient arts. When I am asked why people are so interested in such an inefficient tool as a paddle, I have no pat reply. Possibly I could answer that canoeing, like camping, shooting arrows, and riding horses, is one of the few remaining avenues of escape from efficiency.

Atavistic? Decidedly. But sound.

So much for the versatility, safety, and charm of the canoe. I end this chapter with the *raison d'être* for this book and for all else that I attempt in the educational field.

As a specialist in the uses of natural resources, I had to be a canoeist in order to get around. I likewise had to be a hunter, a horseman, a truck driver, a public speaker, and jack of several other trades in so far as my abilities would permit. A professional conservationist is first an observer, then an interpreter of the environment. But what he can do about his interpretation is often limited by politics, religion, mores, and what-have-you in the realm of human viewpoints.

But tails can wag dogs, and many people can develop an interest in the conservation of natural resources from a non-professional hobby. If a hunter is keen about his sport, he must become a conservationist. If a canoeist gets sufficiently interested, he may become an enthusiast for clean water, sound fish management, good camping conditions, proper forest and watershed protection, and all-around land management.

What's more, anyone who cares about out-of-town diversions—except perhaps the motorist, who moves too rapidly to see much except competing traffic and disfiguring highway signs—is potentially a keen observer. A canoeist is usually such an observer. He notes the beauty, majesty and dignity of natural things; he is appalled by the way in which they can be disfigured through careless exploitation. He knows that, in the world of water, man has made nothing more graceful or more beautiful than a well-handled canoe. It is but a step from liking a graceful and beautiful canoe to demanding a graceful and beautiful environment. This demand, for all its simplicity, can solve most of the natural-resource problems of the whole earth.

And so the canoeist—and with him the hunter, the camper, the field photographer, the cross-country horseman, and all manner of other outdoors enthusiasts —may be the eventual saviors of our land.

2

Canoes—Types and Uses

A canoe may be generally defined as a boat that is *intended* to be paddled rather than rowed. The paddler faces forward and the oarsman faces backward. The oar operates on a fixed fulcrum, and the paddle on a movable fulcrum.

There are exceptions to most rules, and flaws in many definitions. My definition of a canoe is full of flaws. If you put a sail on a canoe, it is still a canoe. It is still a canoe if you put an outboard motor on it. But if you build the craft especially for use with an outboard motor, with a square stern almost as wide as the beam, it may no longer be correctly called a canoe.

On the other hand a Venetian gondola is paddled, and is intended to be paddled; and its upstanding stem and sternpost remind one of the figureheads on West Coast sea-going canoes. But the paddle is oar length, and usually operates on a fixed fulcrum resembling an oarlock. So, a gondola is only a fringe canoe.

2. Aluminum canoe with a narrow stern designed for an outboard motor.

If the definition of a canoe is confusing, definitions of both aboriginal and modern canoes are clear. A reed balsa is a paddle-propelled raft, kept afloat by its buoyant material, and it may be ignored here in spite of its anthropological interest. Actual canoes, as used by aboriginals, fall clearly into two types:

1. Pirogues, or dugouts, made from logs.
2. Framed canoes, covered with bark or skin.

ORIGINAL CANOE TYPES

Log canoes, which we will call pirogues from now on, may have been the first really good small to medium-sized boats used by man. Stone Age people probably made them by burning and scraping; adz-type tools facilitated construction. The details of early pirogues are submerged in the dawn of history, and are purely an ethnological problem which is quite outside the limits of this report.

Modern pirogues are well known, and are fun to make and use if you are skilled and patient, and have a log. I have seen several in the process of being made, and have used several in the Provinces of New Brunswick and Quebec. I have several times talked about making one, but talk is as far as it got.

The materials used in eastern Canada are aspen, white cedar, and white pine. The great sea-going pirogues of the Northwest were all made of western red cedar, and Cajun (Acadian) pirogues of Louisiana were probably made more frequently of bald cypress than of anything else. Anything in the shape of a log that is reasonably easy to work, reasonably free from knots, and not too prone to warp can be made into a pirogue.

The so-called cedars that have been mentioned are among the most workable woods known to science. They are also very durable and very light. Nondurable aspen, however, lasts well in a pirogue, and was preferred by some of the most skilled rivermen I knew in Down East Canada. If aspen is good for this purpose, basswood should be better and tulip poplar better yet, and both of these timbers could be used, one in the North, the other in the South.

South Seas pirogues are made of various woods well known to students of tropical timber, but they need no discussion here. Many of these tropical pirogues are

was made in August, 1914, at Ferme Neuve, Quebec, by Xavier Tenische. Similar canoes are still available if one makes sufficient effort to get them, though both good birch bark and trained Indians are scarcer than they were. When I bought this canoe it cost a dollar a foot.

The largest bark canoe of which I can find an authentic record was described in the *Recollections* of Lieutenant Landman of the British Army. He wrote about his experiences as commander of Fort St. Joseph in 1798. I copy his description exactly as it was quoted in the *Sault Daily Star* (III)* one hundred thirty years later:

"These canoes were exceedingly strong and capacious, they were about thirty-six feet in length, by six wide, near the middle; and although the birch bark which formed thin external coating over their ribs of white cedar, and their longitudinal laths of the same wood, appeared to compose but a flimsy vessel, yet they usually carried a weight of five tons. It may be well to state that this cargo was very carefully stowed, in order to relieve any unequal pressure, which would have been fatal to such a vessel. Four poles, three to four inches in diameter at the thickest ends, denominated by the Canadians, grand perch, and nearly as long as the canoe, were laid side by side in the middle of the bottom of the canoe. On these poles the cargo was carefully arranged, so that all the weight

* Roman numerals in parentheses refer to the Author's Bibliography starting on page 205.

rested on them. . . . Every package was made up to the weight of ninety pounds, and none heavier.

"The five tons included the provision for ten men, sufficient to support them during about twenty to twenty-two days. Each canoe was provided with a mast and lug sail, and also each man had a ten foot setting pole, of good ash, and shod with an iron ferrule at each end, for assisting the men towing with a strong line in ascending the rapids. The paddles were supplied by the canoe men, each bringing also his own. Each canoe had a camp kettle, provided by the owners, as, also, a few Hambro lines, a bundle of wataps, roots of the pine tree, for stitching up any seam that might burst, a parcel of gum of a resinous nature, for paying over the seams when leaky, a piece of birch bark for repairs, hatchet, crooked knife, and a few more indispensable articles.

"The crew consisted of a guide, a steersman, and eight common paddlers, but all worked alike. The guide was paid as much as four ordinary men, and the steersman half as much. Sixteen to twenty pounds was about the wages of a good guide."

The "wataps" were presumably spruce roots rather than pine, and the time the crew worked for such wages is obscure, but it was probably for a month. Twenty pounds was about $100 in 1798, and probably top pay for a guide. This would imply peak wages of $50 for a steersman and $25 for a paddler and packer. You note that "all worked alike." Woodsmen still do.

Times did not change too much from 1798 to 1914.

I was started at $35 a month as a green canoe hand in May of the latter year.

Lieutenant Landman left Montreal on May 12, 1798, in a freight canoe of the type described. He went up the Ottawa, crossed to Lake Nipissing, then down the French River to Georgian Bay in Lake Huron. After getting to the big water, he went up the North Channel to St. Joseph Island.

I have been over some of this route, traveling by canoe, and have examined what is left of Fort St. Joseph. Careful questions suggest that Lieutenant Landman was a conscientious and reasonably observant reporter.

These very large canoes were evidently made by the Ojibways. Mason (II) lists dugouts and rafts as the original craft of the Algonquian-Iroquoian peoples. The big canoes could have been made under the influence of Athapascan-Cree culture, and we know that the Crees were somewhat influenced by the Eskimos. In any event, we will leave much of the rest of canoe history to the historians.

MODERN CANOES

All modern canoes derive from aboriginal prototypes, and instructors frequently state that our cedar-and-canvas canoe is the one thing we have directly inherited from the Indian. I am not at all sure that this is correct, if white man's tools came before good Indian canoes.

We have definitely copied the kayak, but the kayak

is not sufficiently important to rate more than casual
mention here. There is little that you can do with the
kayak that cannot be done more easily with the
ordinary canoe. The kayak, however, can go through
seas that would swamp any other small craft. If the
paddler or paddlers are wedged in the cockpits, and
completely covered with seal-intestine parkas, waves
may sweep right over them with no damage. The fact
that modern kayaks have sailed across the ocean
definitely proves something.

The commonest American canoes of the past generation had "cedar" ribs and planking, and this type
is still in wide use. The eastern white cedar is better
for this than the western red, but the coast white cedar
has sometimes been used and is excellent. The planking is fastened to the ribs with clinched tacks, usually
brass and always rust-proof. The "bark" is deck canvas,
usually No. 8; it is filled, then painted, then varnished.
The finish is discussed in the section on re-covering
(Chap. 4). The gunwales of most of these canoes are
spruce, but sometimes the outwales are oak. The
decks, thwarts, and seats are maple or birch, and the
seats are caned.

I know of few commercial canoes now made shorter
than fifteen feet, none longer than the 35-foot "war"
canoes, and none with greater capacity than a 22-foot
Canadian freighter that will carry two and a half tons.
Greater extremes have existed, and may still exist.

For anything except inter-camp or intercollegiate
racing, I have little interest in war canoes. Freight

canoes or twenty-foot Guide's Special Models are perfectly good for racing, and they are much better for cruising than war canoes.

A half-century ago, all-wood canoes were popular. Peterborough, Ontario, was the home of both the Canadian and the Peterborough Canoe Companies, so the all-wood canoes were sometimes called "Peterboroughs," just as any cowhand's felt hat is sometimes called a "Stetson."

The all-wood canoes were planked with painted basswood, or varnished "cedar" of some sort, over elm ribs. I well remember when racing canoes, like racing shells, were made of the light mahogany commonly called Spanish cedar or cigar-box cedar. But that material has now given place to western red cedar, at least as far as shells are concerned. All-wood canoes are still made, and are beautiful craft. But they require too much care for the casual camper, cruiser, or woods professional. So far as I know they are still used for racing, to the exclusion of other designs.

The all-wood canoe may come closer than any other craft to following the principles of a thin, light pirogue.

There have been two or more efforts to develop all-veneer canoes. These were molded, with no ribs or planking. One that I had a chance to use back in the '20's had a layer of cedar—I assume western red—between two layers of yellow birch. A later veneer canoe that I examined, but did not see taken apart, presumably had some lighter wood between two layers of "mahogany"—probably Philippine mahogany, a fine boat wood not botanically related to the true mahoganies. But I know of no plywood canoes now being made.

Closely related to the plywood jobs, in construction, are the all-metal canoes, usually of aluminum. These canoes are made of two pieces held together by a keel, and are smooth inside. The first canoes of this sort that I saw were in Michigan about 1930. Several manufacturers at least started to make them after 1945. They are popular; as this is written, more aluminum canoes are being sold on this continent than all other types combined. The aluminum craft have the advantage of being a little lighter for their carrying capacity than any of their competitors that I know about. Besides, they need no paint in fresh water, and no housing. An aluminum canoe can lie out the year around without deteriorating much more than an aluminum roof. One disadvantage is that older models *will* sink if bow and stern air chambers become water-logged—though this admittedly is unlikely. And they can be noisy, which at times is a handicap to the hunter.

Aluminum canoes are made in sizes up to 20-foot Guide's Models, but not in actual freight or war-canoe dimensions. I do not like the ultra-light weights. The standard jobs are light enough. Further, due to popular but I feel untutored demand, they are normally made with a deep keel, and you have to pay extra for a low shoe keel.

Aluminum canoes cost a little more than the canvas jobs. They are harder to patch, but they will not puncture as easily on a sharp rock, as the metal is definitely harder than filled canvas. There is little doubt that they will continue to be popular. They deserve their popularity. At the same time cedar-and-canvas has its points.

Canoes of all sorts are now made with open gunwales, so far as I know. Closed gunwales went out for good perhaps thirty years ago, and I have heard of no complaint at their passing.

3

Canoeing Safety

Serious canoeing accidents are rare. You will not be run down by a drunken canoeist! Your canoe will not rear and throw you. You will not have to bail out because power fails, and you can elude many more hazards that unavoidably plague other vocations and sports.

You are, however, dealing with water, and water is a cooperative servant, but—like fire—a harsh master. For that reason some people are afraid of canoes. Certain causes of those fears are considered in Chapter 10. This section emphasizes the very simple methods that can be employed for virtually absolute canoeing safety.

KNOWLEDGE IS SAFETY

In general, a canoeist is safest if he is a good canoeist and has good judgment. We can teach him to be a good canoeist but he must develop his own judgment, and he must depend upon other people's until his own is acquired. That is, unless he depends on luck, and actually is lucky. Luck must not be discounted. You manufacture some of it, but few really active people live to be elderly without admitting that luck is one of the reasons they are still around. It is a poor thing to depend on, however, except in emergencies when you have nothing better. When calculating a risk, you hope for luck, but you don't really count on it.

Knowledge of canoeing promotes canoeing safety just as knowledge of driving promotes motoring safety, good horsemanship promotes riding safety, and so *ad infinitum.* I have been harping on canoeing safety for forty years, just as I have been harping on fire safety in the woods. The National Safety Council and all related organizations harp on all sorts of safety, especially in driving. It does a little good, apparently, so we keep at it.

If you want to go canoeing with safety and good judgment you'll find the following paragraphs worth pondering.

SWIMMING SKILL IS NOT ENOUGH

There may have been unavoidable accidents in which canoeists were saved by swimming. I have never witnessed nor investigated such an accident.

When I first began close association with organized camps, about 1915, many people thought that all one needed to be safe around water was to be a good swimmer. This is not so. I have investigated canoeing accidents in which people drowned, and most of those drowned were good swimmers. In some of them non-swimmers clung to a canoe and were saved, while swimmers swam and died.

Remember the unquestioned fact that few of the northern Canadian professional canoeists can swim a stroke. The Swampy Crees and Yellow Knives of the Barren Grounds, and the Eskimos of the real Arctic Zone, paddle all their lives and never upset. Frequently everything they own is in their canoe, so an accident would mean economic ruin even if they did get out alive.

Now I am all for swimming, when you want to swim. Most young people have been learning to swim for half a century. Progress has been steady and highly commendable. Swimming's fine, in its own time and place. But if you are going out in a canoe with the idea that you'll probably upset but can always swim out of it, my advice is simple. Don't go out!

Commodore Longfellow (XI) as far back as 1930 said:

"It should be emphasized that knowledge of swimming does not give the canoeing student the right to take liberties with his craft. No matter how much of a swimmer he may be, if precipitated into cold water fully dressed, especially after he is fatigued from paddling and hiking, he will probably be unable to swim out. '*Stick to the boat*' is a good motto but the best motto is '*Always avoid an over-turn.*'"

This last ideal, which I italicized, is readily accomplished. In twelve consecutive seasons of organized camp coaching, and in ten other seasons as a staff advisor, I recall only six upsets—I do not refer to stunts —that occurred at camps while I was there.

Two of these upsets happened to girls in fast water. One was in water not over eighteen inches deep. Bad judgment caused the canoe to side-swipe a rock, and it rolled the crew out. In the second instance, a canoe tangled with a fallen tree-top. There was room to clear it, and four out of five canoes did get by. The fifth did not make it, because of faulty steering.

The third to upset was a girl who could not paddle, and who launched a canoe without permission. It was a windy day, and she rolled over not a hundred feet from the dock. She was a swimmer, and she hung on to the canoe until towed ashore.

The other three instances involved boys who upset while playing big fish. They too were excellent swimmers, and were more worried about losing fish and tackle than lives. In their excitement, they forgot to respect their craft's centers of gravity. One of them paid for it with the loss of some valuable tackle.

I know that a combination of canoeing discipline and swimming discipline can *almost* eliminate upsets. I studied the records of the camps I worked for, and some of them (not all) had had occasional upsets before my time. Accidents became very infrequent during my coaching period, but recurred after my departure. This was by no means solely coincidental, admitting that the six upsets that occurred were caused by breaches of discipline or judgment.

In camps, all sorts of accidents should be intolerable, but a few will occur. The campers are all immature, and some of the counselors are green. The American Camping Association safety rules are included in this volume (Appendix), and I am in general agreement with them.

Still, I must reiterate that swimming practice alone, without proper instruction in paddling and watermanship, is dangerous for canoeing. And I cannot forget the "canoe tests" of bygone-days camp, said "canoe tests" consisting of nothing but swimming and upsetting.

To a canoeist, these stunts are comparable to teaching a horseman how to fall off rather than how to ride, a pilot how to bail out rather than how to fly, and a rifleman how to bandage bullet wounds rather than how to shoot. Like swimming stunts, these are all excellent in themselves, but not basic.

A canoeist should be a swimmer, just as a horseman should be skilled in falling. The philosophies, however, are vastly different. I am just as careful a rider as I am a canoeist, but I have never been able to legislate against being "throwed." I am also a careful hunter, but I have never been able to completely avoid the accidental discharge of guns. Nor have I ever met an experienced horseman or experienced shooter who had not suffered the humiliation of falls or accidental discharges. Many experienced canoeists, however—and I am one of them—have never upset a canoe in deep water.

Highway hazards are vaguely similar to canoeing hazards, but greater, in that you may be hit by someone else. There are truck drivers who have driven millions of miles without reportable accidents, and this is the result of their skill and judgment plus a little luck. The canoeist does not usually need luck, but he must have skill, and he must have judgment.

Even so, genuine accidents can happen. It takes a really good man to ride out rough winds and high waves in an open canoe; and to such as are over-bold I frequently quote the last quatrain of William Henry Drummond's *The Wreck of the "Julie Plante"*:

> "De win' can blow lak' hurricane
> An' s'pose she blow some more,
> You can't get drown on Lac St. Pierre
> So long you stay on shore."

I am, unhappily, a poor swimmer and very sensitive to cold water. Many of us old-time canoeists are still around because we knew when to "stay on shore." In some cases our skill—or maybe our luck—got us to shore when the going was rough. Swimming is just great when you want to swim, but it is a poor substitute for canoeing skill and judgment.

Changing Places

In all my canoeing experience, I have never had a real need to change places in a canoe. Even if the steersman should become hopelessly ill, the bow paddler would only have to turn around to take over.

If you do want to change places, all you need to do is limit the motion to one person at a time, keep the center of gravity low, and do not get off balance. Place changing is a valuable balancing stunt that has the same usefulness to a canoeist as the manual of arms has to a soldier. I teach canoeists how to change places because it is customary, but I don't recommend it in big water, far from shore, where upsetting could be serious.

Towing

A towing bridle is illustrated on page 109, and it should be noted that all towing pull should come from a point at, or below the water line.

In general, towing should be limited to empty canoes or dead freight. Under certain circumstances canoes can be towed when lashed together in "teams" with no danger of an upset. It takes skill and experience, however, to get them the right distance apart so that water will not splash in. Further, one freight canoe can frequently tow another. In this case, there should be an alert steersman with paddle in hand in the towed canoe, and an equally alert bow man with a keen knife ready to cut loose.

So far as towing passenger-laden canoes is concerned, I have never known any experienced canoeist who favored it. Still, some New England organized camps made much of this towing at one time, and perhaps still do it. I first saw it done in 1925. The camp by which I was employed had copied this stunt, had had a serious upset, and had nearly drowned a counselor. My director followed my wishes and gave it up. It takes more skill to tow well than it does to paddle well, and so far as I can see, the only reason those being towed were so enthusiastic was because they could not paddle.

There have been some serious towing accidents. I again quote Commodore Longfellow (XI):

"It is always dangerous to tow loaded boats or canoes.

"One of the worst mass drownings in history took place when a string of canoes towed by a motor boat started across Jamaica Bay in a rough sea. Each canoe had two or more passengers. One of the canoes in the front swamped, and in trying to help them, the whole line capsized. Then they commenced to cut loose, it was dark, and help arrived slowly. In the morning there were at least fourteen unclaimed canoes. Several bodies were found lashed to the bell-buoy off Rockaway. They had swum that far and fastened themselves to it. Some excellent rescues were made, but it was a terrible experience, from which we should learn the lesson of never attempting to tow canoes loaded with passengers. Put the passengers in the launch and tow the empty canoes, if you must, and try to get a proper place to make fast to the tow line on the stem at the water line."

Commodore Longfellow reported another towing accident in a Massachusetts lake where nearly twenty boys were drowned.

During certain emergencies I have towed canoes, and have been towed myself. But I put towing a canoe in the same general category as towing a car; you should have a good reason for it, know just what you are doing, and have the proper equipment.

SIMPLE SAFETY DEVICES

Assuming that a canoeist is a good canoeist, accidents will be rare. A good canoeist is always properly equipped, unless he is driven by an emergency and takes a calculated risk. These calculated risks are embarrassing. If someone is in trouble you have to do something if your judgment tells you that possibly you can do it. If your judgment indicates that nothing can be done, trying will only increase the trouble. Blind heroics must be supported by luck or Providence. Possibly both. If one is tossed into the water, a good knowledge of swimming reduces panic and favors rescue, even if there is no need to swim a stroke.

A canoe should never sink. I will never forget a statement by Dr. John B. May, made not later than 1923. He said, "If you hang on to a swamped canoe, you may freeze to death or starve to death, but you will not drown."

The canoeist's worst fear is that in an accident the canoe will get away from him. If it does, he is a swimmer, and nothing but a swimmer. Fully dressed, in big, cold water, he is also likely to be a goner! He has about the same chance as a horseman who is thrown and has one foot hanging in a stirrup. If not knocked unconscious at once, the horseman may climb a bridle or kick loose, but the situation is indeed dire.

In ticklish conditions, I tie my paddle to the canoe with four or five feet of heavy set line. It does not interfere with paddling, and you instinctively hang to the paddle. If you upset or swamp, you have the paddle and can immediately get to the canoe. This is also useful in sport canoeing, in case you must suddenly drop a paddle and grab a gun or a gaff. The late George R. Sears (Nessmuk) was once saved by this simple device.

An equally simple safety device is made by tying cotton rope loops or perhaps bandanna handkerchiefs through the gunwales, so you can hang onto a swamped canoe easily. By thrusting a hand through an eight-inch loop, and then holding the loop, you get a firm hold without being tied so fast that it would be hard to get loose.

I have never needed either of these devices, or any others, but I have been happier a number of times when my canoe was equipped with them.

Nerves

There are some people emotionally unfit to paddle a canoe, or even to ride in anything smaller than a one-ton freighter. Lumpy, over-weight people, with poor muscular coordination, belong on shore or in the care of firm experts. I have guided a couple of lumpy fishermen, and I took a calculated risk for wages!

SENSIBLE CANOEING RULES

Back in 1933 I reported some silly rules posted in the boathouse of a great Midwestern college that is on a beautiful lake and makes much of canoeing. I kept a canoe there myself for a short time, and suffered under those rules. I believe the City Council passed them, and an old lake skipper was entrusted with their enforcement. The rules read more or less as follows, and I hear that twenty years have made little change in them.

1. Each canoeist must have a government-inspected life preserver.
2. Canoes 16 feet or under in length are limited to two passengers.
3. Canoes of 17 feet are limited to three passengers.
4. Canoes over 17 feet in length are limited to four passengers.
5. Canoes are permitted to leave the boathouse only with permission of the boathouse authorities.

These rules seem logical until you inspect them closely. They worked to the extent that drownings were reduced when they were put into effect. As rules, however, they were very poor.

The length of a canoe has very little more relation to its seaworthiness than the length of a rifle barrel has to its range and power. A high-power .30-06 barrel can be cut to twelve-inch length and be very deadly. A 14-foot canoe may also have more carrying capacity than one four feet longer. As American canoes are usually made, one not less than 18 feet long, with 36-inch width and 13-inch depth, or equivalent in displacement, was fit for anyone to use on that big, windy lake. My Canadian 16-foot Prospector Model would have done well enough. I never saw a canoe shorter than 16 feet on this lake.

There was no regulation about rope loops or tied paddles. The life preservers produced a measure of safety, but they alone could not keep a crew from being scattered. If four paddlers upset, it is a good idea to find them all with the canoe when help arrives. Hunting scattered victims is embarrassing. I have done it.

It is sound to prohibit canoeing in dangerous weather, but instruction rather than policing bears the most fruit. Most of the people who used that boathouse had had no instruction.

RESCUE OF SWIMMERS

In some places canoes are the only lifeboats available, and must be used to rescue all sorts of water victims. It should be noted that any canoe with the displacement of my 16-foot Prospector or bigger is a good enough emergency lifeboat. We are making an educational picture for the Idaho State College library, and using my canoe for that purpose.

A light life ring with plenty of quarter-inch rope helps in any sort of rescue, but we have occasionally dragged tired swimmers into canoes, and greased swimmers at that, without shipping much water. Practice will usually develop the easiest techniques, and the bigger the canoe the easier the job. In an 18-foot freighter or a larger craft, you may stand up and drag a swimmer in, just as you drag one over the stern of a lifeboat. A canoe has the advantage over a rowboat in that the paddlers face forward, and can approach the subject more precisely than oarsmen. A square-stern Canadian freighter, paddled stern first, may be an ideal rescue canoe, but a 20-foot Guide's Special is good enough.

4

Canoeing Strokes

I earned wages in a canoe for several seasons before I heard any canoe stroke called much of anything, and I got along fine. When I started in as a bow man, my steersman might say, "Edge 'er left a little," or "Swing maybe fifteen degrees right." Perhaps he might add, "I could use a faster stroke," or in certain types of water, "They might be slower and longer." But that was all.

Still, names do help in large-scale instruction, and in written descriptions like this, so we have to have them. There has been some confusion as to stroke names in the forty years that I have been a critical observer of canoeing, and I feel that canoeists should work toward such simple designations as the "walk," "trot," and "lope" of a horse that is "three-gaited." Of course you can argue about a "running walk," and just where a "lope" becomes a "gallop," and a "gallop" a "run." And you can get hopelessly confused if you try to work out all the gaits of our pronghorn antelope. He has all the five gaits of a five-gaited horse and several more of his own. Trying to analyze all of them would be amusing, if you had lots of time, but the antelope would not travel better after your analysis. He travels all right as he is.

Later in this chapter I shall discuss current stroke nomenclature in some detail, for the benefit of those who are familiar with the usually accepted terms and definitions. But first, I shall describe the very few basic strokes, and how to execute and use them.

BASIC PADDLING STROKES

The simplest method I have found to explain basic paddling strokes is to compare them to the four cardinal directions in which you can walk: forward, backward, sideways to the right, and sideways to the left. In terms of paddling, we thus have the following:

1. A simple *forward* stroke, that shoves the canoe ahead and swings the *bow* of the craft *away* from the paddling side.

2. A *backward* stroke, that moves the canoe astern while swinging the bow *toward* the paddle.

3. A *draw* stroke, that pulls the canoe *toward* the paddle. When the paddle is used on the *left* side, the draw moves the canoe toward the left; on the right side it, of course, pulls the canoe toward the right. If this stroke is used by a single paddler in the middle

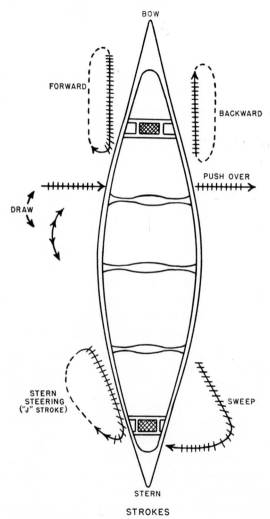

BOW

FORWARD

BACKWARD

PUSH OVER

DRAW

STERN
STEERING
("J" STROKE)

SWEEP

STERN

STROKES

4. Patterns of principal paddle strokes.

of the canoe, the craft moves broadside; if used at one end only, it is that end which moves the most.

4. A *push-over* stroke, that pushes the canoe away from the paddle. It is the exact opposite of the draw.

Since there are only these four basic directions, there are only four basic strokes. This is important in teaching, as you can use the cardinal points of the compass, the handling of a horse, the manipulation of a car, or many other things for comparison.

If we can agree on these four basic directions and four basic strokes, we should also agree that a *combination* of *two* strokes (rarely of three) can make the canoe go in any direction chosen by the skilled paddler. Hence there is some question as to whether or not it is necessary to name any other strokes. Two of the combinations are so purposeful, however, that I will name and number them as follows:

5. A *stern steering* stroke, that makes the canoe move forward while holding the bow on the same point, although the wake is curved. This is a combination of forward and push-over, and is frequently called a "J" stroke.

6. A *sweep* stroke, that moves the bow swiftly away from the paddling side. In the bow, it is done through an arc of 90°, and is a combination of push-over and forward. In the stern, where it is done through 180°, it starts as a push-over plus forward, operates briefly as a simple forward, and ends mainly as a draw. This is one of the instances in which three basic-direction strokes are usable in combination.

DESCRIPTION OF BASIC STROKES

For elementary purposes, we will assume that you are equipped with a single-blade paddle, and are using it on one side of the canoe only. Your upper hand grasps the paddle naturally, fingers forward over the knob. Your lower hand is placed about two inches above the blade, and your thumb should be on the *outside* of the shaft to prevent its being banged against the gunwale. The majority of untrained people take hold of a paddle in proper form as a matter of course, except that they encircle it with the lower thumb. This is a matter of choice. If you are determined to knock your thumbnail off on a gunwale, your instructor should warn you but not insist, unless you are very young. You kneel in the canoe, knees spread at least fifteen inches, and lean comfortably against a seat or thwart.

In all the basic strokes needed to impart forward or sideward motion, *the lower arm is usually kept rather straight.* In all of them except the draw, the recovery or finish of the stroke is always executed with the *inside edge* (edge of blade toward canoe) turned *toward the stern.* This is the first point on which the instructor should bear down, and many beginning canoeists do not seem to grasp it easily. You cannot steer properly, paddle bow properly, or do anything else properly except the draw, if the outside edge of the paddle is turned toward the stern at the finish of the stroke.

Here it may be well to note that the paddling developed by primitive people involves the absolute minimum in motion and effort. Aboriginals are either lazy or efficient, if these terms are not synonymous. Every teacher of physical skills is concerned with maximum efficiency. Every motion in paddling must be so analyzed and taught as to take full advantage of leverage, gravity, friction, and all other physical and mechanical forces. I have done that in my selection of strokes, and in the directions for doing them. If I have sacrificed power, as in denying a circling-thumb grip by the lower hand, I have done it to save probable thumb damage. If you have a nail knocked off, you lose more efficiency than you could gain through a grip one percent stronger.

It is possible for an otherwise uninstructed person to learn to paddle in perfect form from written and diagramed instructions. This demands meticulous attention, but it can be done. Moving pictures add to this instruction, and my wife and myself were the subjects of an educational film on paddling now in the library of Idaho State College.

But, admitting the value of directions, diagrams, and educational films, a good coach is better. The trick is to find a good coach. There has been considerable faulty coaching in the past, and it may or may not have been entirely eliminated as this edition goes to the press. I refer to the type of coaching that will not meet the standards of the professional Canadian guide, Indian, Eskimo, African, South Sea Islander, or other native who uses a canoe in the business of living. All of them, including the gondolier, use a paddle in essentially the same way. A good paddler is a good paddler anywhere in the world, just as a good swimmer, a good runner, a good shot, or a good horseman is good anywhere. Equipment varies, but a jockey can learn to use a stock saddle in about ten minutes. Similarly an Ojibway could make a gondola sit up and beg if he were turned loose on the Grand Canal. His ability in either Italian vituperatives or music might be scant, and so might mine, but either of us could handle the gondola.

1. *The Forward Stroke*

Most right-handed people naturally paddle with greater ease on the left side of the canoe. Mrs. Jarvis' diagram shows this most important stroke operating on the left.

Your paddle for ordinary forward paddling should be six inches shorter than your height if you are of average stature, but it should rarely be shorter than five feet or longer than five feet nine inches. The lower part of its shaft should be wrapped to prevent wear on the gunwale.

You grasp the paddle with the left hand near the blade, thumb outside for reasons stated. Your left arm should be straight but not stiff, and *that left arm stays straight in all ordinary forward paddling*. It does not bend at any time or place during the execution of the stroke. Your right hand, holding the paddle by the knob, is back within a few inches of your right shoulder. You have taken the kneeling position already described.

From this stance, you sway forward slightly from the hips and dip the paddle squarely in the water, a convenient distance from the canoe. As soon as the paddle starts into the water it is drawn back by the left hand, and at the same time the right arm straightens, swinging a little to the left with a powerful triceps thrust. The body sways slightly backward during the stroke.

When the paddle reaches the end of a convenient stroke, the *inside edge* of the blade is turned sharply to the stern by means of a slight out-flexing of both wrists. Then the right hand is sharply depressed to the right, and the paddle comes out of the water, the blade parallel to the surface. It is brought out partly by a right (upper) hand pry, and partly by a left (lower) hand lift.

As soon as the paddle is clear of the water, it is brought forward for the next stroke, feathered parallel to the surface and as close to it as may be without hitting it and "crabbing." When the paddle gets as far forward as is convenient, the blade is swiftly turned so that it is perpendicular to the water, the bent right arm straightens, and the stroke is repeated.

There are certain modifications in the forward stroke, applying to certain special conditions, which I will mention later. But this stroke, exactly as described, should be mastered first.

All ordinary strokes are executed in the same way as the forward stroke, so far as sitting position, paddle grasp, and general physical principles are concerned. As soon as any stroke is fairly well developed on one side of the canoe, the student should change sides. No one *should* develop a favorite paddling side, but the majority do acquire a one-side habit.

2. *The Backward Stroke*

The backward stroke, or backwater if you wish, is shown on the right side in the basic stroke diagram. It is done exactly like the preceding stroke in reverse, with the exception that the lower arm is *not* kept straight. In fact both elbows may be more or less flexed throughout the stroke.

Keep especially in mind that, in recovery, the *inside edge* of the paddle is turned toward the stern exactly as in the forward stroke.

Do not have the slightest concern as to where the canoe goes while the forward and backward strokes are being learned. In the first the bow will swing away from the paddle, in the second toward it. But the strokes can be learned in a canoe, in an anchored barge or rowboat, or while sitting on a dock. We are primarily concerned with proper motions.

3. *The Draw Stroke*

In the draw you reach out to the side, blade parallel to the keel, and pull the canoe toward the paddle. This stroke has, correctly enough, been called the "pull-to." When the paddle gets close to the canoe, you knife it out of the water, and reach for another stroke. As easy as that!

It is neater, but slightly less powerful, to recover by not taking the paddle out of the water at all, but instead, turning it edgewise (toward whichever edge you find handiest), knifing it out to a convenient spot, then turning it flat and pulling it in again.

A third and still neater draw could be called a *sculling draw,* and is simply named "sculling" in some manuals. It is done by reaching out a convenient distance, keeping the blade almost parallel to the keel, and then whipping it right and left in swift, flat arcs. Most of the pressure is applied by the lower hand. The blade stays about the same distance from the canoe, and the canoe walks toward it. This is very easy to demonstrate and to learn.

4. The Push-over Stroke

Next to the simple forward stroke, the push-over is the most important. Few paddlers pick it up without some sort of instruction, and some well-known coaches teach it improperly, according to most woodsmen's standards. Starting from the same initial stance, paddle grasp, and position as for forward paddling—in this instance our diagram shows the paddle operating at the right—the procedure is as follows:

Rest the paddle *edgewise* (blade perpendicular to the keel) on the gunwale of the canoe. Knife it into the water until the left hand is above the gunwale, the shaft of the paddle still touching the gunwale. By this time the shaft of the paddle is perpendicular to the surface of the water, or almost perpendicular. Then swiftly turn the left hand, wrist out, until the blade is parallel to the keel. At the same moment pry down with the left hand, holding the shaft of the paddle lightly against the gunwale with the right. The canoe dips slightly toward the paddle during this simple pry. The stroke is rapidly repeated in order to achieve maximum efficiency. The recovery is usually under water, the shaft of the paddle staying in one spot on the gunwale.

Properly done, this is the most powerful stroke in canoeing, as it is straight levering. The gunwale is the fulcrum, and the left hand furnishes the prying power. Now the lever is a very strong mechanism, so care must be taken not to smash a paddle when the canoe is so heavily loaded that it does not "give" readily.

Again, note that the *inside edge* of the paddle is turned toward the stern while doing this stroke. There is reason for this. This stroke as I describe it is most valuable because it is taught immediately before the stern steering stroke—which is a but slightly modified combination of push-over and forward stroke.

None the less, some well-known coaches turn the *outside edge* of the blade to the stern in teaching the push-over. With this technique, of course, the teaching sequence is completely shattered. Further, very powerful leverage is easy with the stroke as I describe it, because the weight of the hand and arm is smashing the lever down. With the blade turned the other way, the power is limited to a much weaker finger pull.

Note, too, that the paddle works against the gunwale during this stroke. A generation ago, I knew paddling instructors who had temper tantrums if a student touched the shaft of his paddle to the gunwale. They claimed it was wrong to do so, but they gave no valid reasons as to why it was wrong.

5. The Stern Steering Stroke

In executing this stroke it is usually best to use a paddle that is within three inches of the height of the paddler. The average man will generally use a five-and-a-half-foot paddle, and the average woman will use one three inches shorter.

You dip the paddle exactly as in the ordinary forward stroke. You turn it exactly as in the forward stroke—except that, as you turn the inside edge to the rear, you hold the shaft against the gunwale and lever the stern away from the paddle as the blade cuts out of the water. It is simply a combination of forward and push-over. But take care to bring the paddle out of the water with a *convex* (*not* concave) arc. And don't be in too much of a hurry to get the paddle turned for the next dip.

In further analysis, the "forward" beginning of the stern steering stroke tends to push the canoe forward, but swings the bow away from the paddling side. The push-over finish shoves the stern away from the paddle, and since the bow and stern are (we hope) irrevocably tied together, the bow swings back *toward* the paddle. When a single paddler is handling a canoe, this movement of bow and stern makes a wake that is curved, and curved away from the paddling side.

I have heard some instructors separate the stern steering stroke into a "fore stroke" that shoves the canoe forward but bends the bow out of a straight line, and a "back stroke" that straightens it out. But further demonstration will show that the leverage of the push-over finish, or "back stroke" portion, also moves the canoe forward.

The paddling student should also note that the stern paddler can vary this stroke in many ways. He can put a lot of push-over on the end of it and swing the bow hard toward his paddle. Or he can ease the push-over and drift the bow away from his paddle. And by combining a draw with a forward stroke, he can swing the bow away from the paddling side very sharply.

Since so many modifications are possible in steering, I have certain misgivings in giving it separate stroke status. However the so-called "J" stroke, which I first heard named in 1919, has achieved such popularity or notoriety that something is needed to replace what it more or less represents, if this "J" is abandoned by name.

The "Canadian chop," in case you have heard of it, is simply a hard, fast application of the stern steering stroke. It was frequently used by Canadian woodsmen some forty years ago.

6. *The Sweep Stroke*

This combination stroke got its name because it is used to turn the bow swiftly away from the paddle by a sweeping motion. In the stern, it is done through a slightly angular half-circle, about as one would use a broom to whoosh the chickens off the back porch. It begins far forward, and includes certain modifications of pushing over, paddling forward, and drawing, mostly the first and the last. In the bow it is done through not more than a quarter-circle, and is a combination of a delicately modified push-over, without gunwale leverage, and a forward stroke.

Some Other Combination Strokes

The meaning of the command "hold" is so obvious that little explanation is needed. You stick your paddle in the water, the blade perpendicular to the way you are going, and you immediately slow up.

You can paddle a canoe to the rear at any angle you wish by means of a backward stroke combined with a draw to either the right or the left of the stern.

It is very neat to scull a canoe forward, in exactly the same way that a rowboat is propelled forward with a single oar operated over the stern. Sculling in this way, with the paddle blade of course staying under water, is very useful in sneaking up on game. Many duck boats on the Mississippi in the Tri-cities area are known as "scull boats," and I have carefully studied their operation. The physical principle is very close to that employed in our stern steering, but the stroke is much shortened and the blade stays under water.

This, by far the most important part of the text, may be closed by emphasizing that a canoe un-hampered by wind or current can be made to go almost anywhere by a single paddle operated from any point in it, if it is so ballasted that its full length is in the water. Even a single paddler in the bow can bow-steer almost straight ahead by combining his forward stroke with a draw—exactly opposite to the stern steering operation, which combines a forward stroke with a push-over.

The steersman's position in the canoe will alter his stroke execution slightly. If he sits on the stern, he will pry across his leg, not on the gunwale, in pushing over. If he stands, and he often will in very fast water, the situation is not especially altered, admitting that in fast water—to be gone into in more detail later—the bow paddler does most of the steering.

Double-blade work is briefly described in Chapter 7.

Finally, the student is cautioned not to take stroke names too seriously—not even mine, although they are the simplest and clearest that I know, and were decided upon only after long deliberation and consultation. As I indicated earlier, other systems of stroke nomenclature are used in the official booklets of several different organizations concerned with canoeing. One of these diagrams ten strokes, and illustrates an eleventh in a photograph. A second lists ten bow and four stern strokes, mentioning that five of the bow strokes can be used in the stern too. All of these strokes, which by no means exhaust the number that could be differentiated, are correctly described. But in my opinion it is needlessly confusing to distinguish and teach so many strokes. Besides, some of them are misleadingly named. My viewpoint, which may be of interest to experienced canoeists, is explained in the section which follows: and I suggest that readers who are unfamiliar with current nomenclature should skip to the next chapter.

COMPARISON OF DUPLICATE STROKE NAMES

1. My *forward* stroke is the same as the *bow* stroke described in some manuals. There is no disagreement on how to do it; but I object to the name "bow stroke" because it can—and does—imply that the stroke is to be used primarily in the bow. This is not so. It may be used by a paddler anywhere, including the stern, if there is no occasion to use a modified combination of forward and push-over for steering.

2. My *backward* stroke is the same as the *backwater* of other writers. There is scant confusion here. In crew commands, the term "back" is the common expression.

3. *Draw*, as I use it, indicates three slightly different strokes, as previously described. The official classifications of several organizations agree with me, with one exception mentioned in paragraph 7 below.

4. *Push-over*, as I use the term, is sometimes called

the "pry" stroke. It is agreed upon with few modifications.

5. My *stern steering* stroke is generally called the "J" stroke—and this term "J" has caused more confusion than any other in the whole lexicon of canoeing. The name, which arose with a style of stern paddling that I first saw in 1919, was supposed to indicate the path described in the water by the paddle as the stroke was executed on the left side of the canoe. (In paddling on the right, the "J" would be reversed.) Actually, when you paddle correctly, the path of your paddle resembles a "J" only remotely. It is more nearly a "V," but a "V" with a slightly rounded base, both sides curved, and one shank longer than the other. Originally, the stroke was more fully described as the "straight-arm J." It was a product of the school of thought which held that, in proper paddling form, neither elbow should ever be bent. Stiff-arm paddling, as a generally taught method, has now largely passed into Limbo, and I should like to see this name go with it.

6. *Sweep* stroke is agreed upon and is not confusing.

7. *Sculling,* as the term is employed in several official sets of canoeing instructions, is about as ambiguous a word as you can find. As ordinarily understood in common English, it means propelling a boat by a single oar or paddle worked over the stern, and this is the sense in which I used the word earlier in this chapter. It can also mean handling a light racing shell

with paired oars, a definition obviously without relevance to canoeing. But some of the canoeing manuals use it as the name for one of the several draw strokes—the third of those I have already described. The stroke is very useful. The name "sculling," as applied to it, is not; it is most confusing. If a separate name is wanted for this type of draw stroke, I suggest that *sculling draw* would be the most satisfactory.

8. *Reverse sculling*, defined as the opposite of the "sculling draw" I have just been discussing, is used to throw the canoe away from the paddle, and is thus a form of push-over. It will do nothing that an ordinary push-over will not do better, and I consider it a totally useless stunt stroke, which we may as well consign to oblivion along with the straight-arm "J."

9. *Bow-rudder*, as described in one publication, is used to draw the canoe toward the paddle. It is in reality a slight modification of a forward stroke combined with a draw, and I do not think it deserves the dignity of a separate name.

10. *Cross bow-rudder* is described as the above, done without changing hands on the side opposite to that on which you are paddling. I know of nothing it will do that a push-over will not do better.

At one time a stroke called the "cross-bow" was taught, and back in 1924 I saw its most enthusiastic promoter fall out in demonstrating it. It was useless then, and is equally useless now, except as a stunt. However, there is, very rarely, an occasion where a stroke that could be called the "cross draw" is useful.

11. *Hold* is listed as a stroke by some writers, and certainly it is a useful position but I feel it is not quite a stroke. It consists of holding the blade rigidly in the water, and is generally used to retard forward motion. In this case, since you must stop the canoe before you can back it, the hold is in reality a modification of the backward stroke. You can, of course, hold equally well to prevent the craft from going backward or sideward, and these "strokes" could be called quiescent modifications of the forward stroke, the draw, and the push-over.

Though I have heard several other stroke names used, they are not sufficiently emphasized in current literature to rate discussion here.

5

The Selection of Canoeing Equipment

As I remarked earlier, cedar-and-canvas canoes and aluminum models are the most popular at present. We can ignore rubber rafts completely, as they are not remotely considered canoes. A brief discussion of kayaks is included with data on double-blade paddling in Chapter 7.

There are a few inflatable canoes, and folding canvas models also. They are handled the same as any other canoes. They have one advantage and one only: you can pack them on a horse or in a crowded plane. Any ordinary canoe will submit gracefully to travel by car, trailer, truck, ship, train, or human back.

Right now aluminum canoes are outselling all others, and they have their advantages. They never have to be painted if used in fresh water, and they need no housing.

Further, aluminum canoes are a little lighter than canvas models of the same capacity. The extra-light ones are considerably lighter, but much weaker than the standard weights. There are admittedly occasions when extra-light canoes have an advantage, but I will not dwell on them. I consider them in the same category as extra-light guns. Both are usually unnecessary and unsatisfactory.

The chief disadvantage of aluminum canoes is that they are noisier in the water, a factor to be considered by the sportsman, as I show in Chapter 9. But my greatest complaint about them is that I do not like their looks! None the less I plan to get one—a twenty-footer. Canvas and aluminum canoes are about the same price.

The canvas canoe is more buoyant. Its materials are themselves lighter than water, and it will stay afloat even when filled to the gunwales. A swamped canvas canoe would float you to shore from the middle of Lake Superior.

If I were outfitting a camp with new canoeing equipment, I would shop for values. Further, I would definitely want examples of both canvas and aluminum canoes. No one should have any trouble with either. Among United States canoes, however, the 20-foot aluminum job is the only *really* big one I know about that is built for general cruising.

DIMENSIONS AND DISPLACEMENT

In a long-discontinued publication (IV) I listed in 1928 what I then believed to be the dimensions of a perfect camp canoe. It was the low-bow Chestnut

Cruiser model. It was 18 feet long, 34 inches wide on the gunwales and spreading to 36 inches in the "tumble home," and 13 inches deep amidship. It had three thwarts and two seats. Both ribs and planking were white cedar. Its weight was about 80 pounds.

In the quarter century that has elapsed between that writing and this, I have found no reason to change the description of my ideal camp canoe. The United States Guide's Models (the Chestnut is Canadian made) are very nearly of the dimensions listed, though the Guide's Models are 18½ rather than 18 feet long.

My 16-foot Prospector Model, made by the Canadian Canoe Company of Peterborough, Ontario, and the only canoe I own at present, is a full 36 inches wide and 14 inches deep. It has at least as much carrying capacity as the 18-foot cruiser or Guide's Model, and it is a little more seaworthy, a little stronger, and a few pounds heavier. Being shorter, it is a little slower to paddle. Within certain limits, the longer, slimmer, and lighter a canoe is, the easier it is to handle. Nothing handles better than an 18-footer if you have sea room. A 16-footer is better in twisting rapids, and just possibly a 14-footer is better yet if you are exclusively concerned with rapids. But, unless your needs are highly specialized, you will never want a canoe smaller than 16 feet by 34 inches by 12 inches in dimensions, and 65 pounds in weight.

I worked for a couple of camps that had Guide's

Models measuring 20 feet by 36 inches by 14 inches, and weighing a hundred pounds. They were great trip canoes for parties of four. Even with young campers and a counselor in each craft, there was plenty of space for duffel. A good packer can carry one of these canoes alone for a reasonable distance.

Though real freight canoes are not made in this country, I assume because there is not sufficient demand, Canadian freighters of medium size are *very* useful. The two best sizes are 18 feet by 46 inches by 18 inches, weight 130 pounds, capacity 1600 pounds; and 19 feet by 51 inches by 21 inches, weight 160 pounds, capacity 2000 pounds.

These big canoes are fine for sailing, they are available with square sterns for motors, and they are still fairly easy to paddle. But they cannot be had in this country without paying a heavy duty import. The nearest United States substitute is the already mentioned Grumman 20-foot aluminum canoe, which has a capacity close to that of the 18-foot freighter and weighs about 115 pounds. It is much easier to paddle, and not quite as seaworthy. However canoes no more seaworthy have been paddled the whole length of Lake Superior. You have to use discretion.

We might summarize by stating that few people, anywhere, need a canoe shorter than 16 feet or longer than 20 feet. No 16-foot canoe should be narrower than 34 inches, shallower than 12 inches, or lighter than 65 pounds. Guide's Models 18, 18½, or 20 feet long are the most satisfactory canoes for camping,

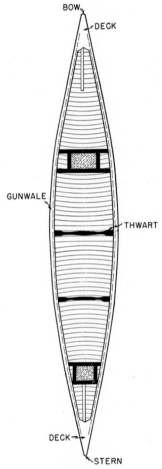

BOW

DECK

GUNWALE

THWART

DECK

STERN

5. Common canvas canoe design, 20-foot Guide Special proportions.

fishing, hunting and cruising that are available in this country. The biggest aluminum canoes are the most seaworthy of any now made here. War canoes will not tip easily, but high waves swamp them.

For most purposes, too many people are too anxious to use light canoes. This is partially the fault of the manufacturers, who want to make everything easy for the customer. If the customer drowns, however, he will never buy anything else. It is desirable to keep him alive as well as happy.

If you have a camp and can afford a lot of canoes, get several sizes. They all have their places. Unless you are getting some war canoes, however, stick to lengths of 16, 18 (or 18½), and 20 feet.

Gunwales and Thwarts

At one time canoes were made with both "open" and "closed" gunwales. Closed gunwales have not been made, so far as I know, for a long time, so there is no longer a problem of choice.

Most canvas canoes are ordinarily manufactured with both inwales and outwales made of spruce. Spruce outwales splinter easily. You can get outwales in oak at slight extra cost, and they add very little to the craft's weight. They are much more satisfactory.

Thwarts in aluminum canoes are aluminum, and do well enough. Canvas canoe thwarts are always made of satisfactory hardwood (yellow birch is hard to beat) so there is little complaint regarding their material.

In most canoes which have two seats, the front seat takes the place of the front thwart, there is a middle thwart, and the rear thwart is in front of the rear seat. Ignoring seats (and Indians really ignored them!) the average canoe of 18 feet or less has three thwarts, one in the middle, the others evenly proportioned fore and aft.

If you ask canoe manufacturers to do so, they will put the thwarts anywhere you want them, and some instructors do not like the standard thwart arrangement. I have no complaint about it, nor have I known the best Canadian woodsmen to complain about it. With standard thwarts, I have—apparently—been able to go anywhere that anyone could go, either alone or with a crew.

If you find a good reason for changing the position of the thwarts after you have given the standard arrangement a thorough trial, do so by all means. Otherwise leave it alone. I put a carrying yoke in place of the middle thwart, but make no other changes.

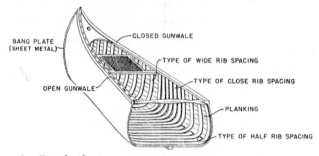

6.   Details of canoe construction.

Ribs

There used to be some arguments about ribbing. Aluminum canoes have no ribs. Canvas canoes have ribs which taper toward the gunwales, and are spaced about their own width apart. Ribs should always be made of eastern white cedar instead of western red cedar.

Some canoes have been built with half-ribs, thus making an almost solid bottom. These half-ribs cause a zone of weakness at their ends, and weaken a canoe more than they strengthen it.

Canadian canoes can be had close-ribbed if you order them that way. Probably American canvas-canoe builders would give you close ribbing if you asked for it and paid the price. If—as sometimes is the case— western red cedar ribs are used, closer ribbing adds to the durability of the canoe.

Stem Bands or Bang Plates

Canvas canoes are made with metal strips attached to the outside curve of bow and stern, covering the tacked-down ends of the canvas and protecting the ends of the craft. Manufacturers often call these "bang plates," but the name does not imply that you can "bang" them with impunity.

Bands of sheet brass riveted around the stems are the best protection for canvas canoes. If you are using an American-made canvas canoe, I suggest that you demand them. They are available at this writing and have been as long as I can remember. My only objection to them is that they are hard to take off and put on.

All the aluminum canoes are manufactured with sheet metal stem bands as an integral part of their structure.

Planking

Aluminum canoes obviously are not planked, but canvas canoes are. Eastern white cedar is the best wood for this purpose, but little if any is now going into United States-made canoes. You are lucky to get eastern cedar ribs, let alone planking.

We are frequently asked what, if any, are the advantages of planking with pieces that run the full length of the canoe. Admittedly a lot of joints are no advantage. But if the joints of the planks are properly staggered, and properly fastened with well-clinched brass tacks, the lengths of the pieces are not too important. Most canoes are well planked in these particulars.

More important than plank length is careful fitting. One manufacturer bevels and laps each strip, so that the inevitable swelling and shrinking of the cedar opens fewer cracks and permits less rubbish to get between the planks and the canvas. It happens that this manufacturer is the same one who supplies sheet metal stem bands as standard equipment, and these two features alone have put him high in the opinion of professional canoeists. But please do not assume that any standard canoes are poor. They are all good —just as all standard automobiles are good, to make a horrible comparison!—and few canoeists are remotely as good as the canoes they paddle.

Bows and Sterns

Unless it is especially designed for use with a motor, the canoe's two ends are exactly alike. You paddle it either way you wish. There are differences in end designs. There are also, high, low, and torpedo bows.

If the canoe is to be used in open water, the low

bow is an advantage. The high bow and the torpedo bow, though possibly useful in rapids to keep water from splashing in, may well be forgotten here. If you are a sufficiently expert canoeist to know when a high-bow canoe (if you can find one) will be an advantage, you do not need to study this book. The matter may thus be settled in favor of the standard low bow for general purposes.

Seats

There are arguments about seats. I have never seen a seat in an Indian-made canoe. An Indian probably would sit on the seats of a "paleface canoe" if it seemed logical, but he would never consider them important enough to put in a canoe he was making for himself.

In teaching young paddlers, I insist that they kneel. If there are no seats it saves foolish questions. In a canoe as big as my 16-foot Prospector, however, I prefer seats. It is safe to sit on a canoe seat when it is safe to sit on one! It is also safe to stand when it is safe to stand. You had better know. Until you know, you had better kneel. I repeat that dangerous matters, including deep water, lethal weapons, and matrimony, all involve calculated risks. As little as possible should be left to luck.

I rarely sit on a canoe seat. If I am in the condition that I should be in, I can kneel all day. For practice canoes, I definitely prefer no bow seat. If a canoe is made with no seats, I am Indian enough never to put any in. If seats are built in, I am paleface enough never to take them out.

If there are seats in a canoe, they should be flush with the gunwales and not down-hung. If they are down-hung, I change them. They must not be too low to lean on comfortably. A low front seat, to *make* the bow paddler sit low, is largely a delusion. The stern seat should be placed as far back as it can go. The biggest advantage of a stern seat is that, from it, you can get up to stand more easily than you can from your knees. At least I can. To look rapids over, you frequently must stand.

There are places for seatless canoes. But sweeping statements as to Indians disliking them are open to question. The politician who brags that he was born in a cabin with a dirt floor may definitely prove his pioneer stock. If he comes from wooded country, however, he may also prove that his papa was too lazy or too unskilled to hew a floor. Natives are frequently beautiful canoeists, but their selection of equipment may be the result of habits, styles and ambitions rather than conscious choice. We are all much the same.

Keels

Keels—ordinary deep keels—are very popular, and many people feel that a canoe is "safer" if it wears a keel. There is no doubt that a keel adds slightly to the lateral stability of a canoe, because it makes the bottom less slippery. The size and construction of the canoe, however, have a lot more than the keel to do with its stability. No canoes of the sizes recommended in recent pages—that is, 16 feet by 34 inches by 12 inches, or greater—would be measurably stabilized by keels.

Still, on canoes to be used *exclusively* on lakes, and *never* in fast water, an ordinary deep keel is an advantage. Keeled canoes hold better in the wind. But on

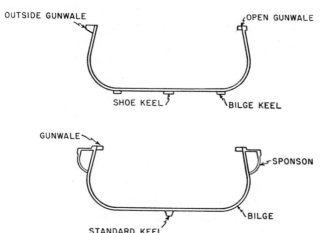

7.   Sections of canoes.

canoes to be used in fast water, a keel is dangerous. As soon as it gets out of parallel with the direction of flow, the current's influence is vastly increased. Keeled canoes have frequently been damaged in rapids, where keelless canoes would have escaped safely.

Some excellent guides will not use a keel-equipped passenger canoe for any purpose, except in a dire emergency. This is partly the result of a combination of pride and prejudice. A keeled canoe, in the woods where I have worked, is considered as unprofessional as a safety razor in a barber shop.

The flat shoe keel is a compromise. It protects the bottom of the canoe admirably, but does not interfere with fast-water handling. Excellent Canadian professionals, who have no use for keels, admit that they cannot find anything wrong with the way a shoe-keeled canoe handles in fast water.

Shoe keels on canvas canoes are about two inches wide and three-eighths of an inch deep. They are made of fine-grained hardwood, usually birch. Shoe keels on aluminum canoes are half round, and are simply reasonably flat devices to hold the craft together. They are not standard equipment, but have to be ordered specially at higher cost.

All the real freight canoes that I have seen have been equipped with rather heavy keels for bracing as well as for protection. The heaviest models also have bilge keels, or wearing strips screwed on parallel to the main keel. On six of these, a 300-pound canoe can be dragged over the beach without hurting it much. Considering that these arks must frequently be beached with up to their full 5,000-pound load, this bottom protection is essential. Their stability is not appreciably increased by these keels. They are very stable anyway.

My final suggestion is to insist on no keel or a shoe keel if you are ever going to use your canoe on a river. You can use keelless canoes well on lakes. If deep keels for canoes had never been devised, no professional would worry. No Indian ever remotely considered putting a keel on his canoe. Maybe, in fairness to the keel boosters, we could admit that putting on a keel would have been too much work!

Sponsons

If the professional canoeist is vexed by old wives' tales about the safety of deep keels, he is enraged by sponsons. These are narrow floats, built lengthwise onto each side of the canoe above the water-line. They are either solid hunks of very light wood or block cork, or air tanks. The latter are now more common.

Some people like sponsons—claim they are "safer," they add to the stability of the craft, they will not sink. Actually, sponsons do absolutely nothing to stability that simple width doesn't do as well. If a canoe is 38 inches wide, sponsons included, a 38-inch canoe without sponsons would be just as stable, and easier to handle. As to non-sinking qualities, any canvas canoe when awash will float more people than can safely ride in it when it is dry. It is thus buoyant enough, and adding more buoyancy is gilding an already adequate lily.

Sponson canoes are much heavier, size for size, than the standard models. They are consequently less responsive, and far less fun to handle. But perhaps the worst thing about them is that they give a false feeling of safety to the timid and untutored. Like a sack of assafoetida and camphor hung around the neck, as a substitute for smallpox vaccination.

Back in the '20's I worked for a canoe-timid girls'-camp director who had a private sponson canoe. She used it on the rare occasions when she risked the waves of her very small and safe lake, perhaps three times in the two-month camp season. She did not quite trust the canoes that she bought for the use of her paying guests and faithful employees.

No one else wanted to use this sponson job. It was heavy and clumsy. Its privacy was thus assured. Further, since neither its owner nor any of the damsels was strong enough to get it in or out of the water, it stayed afloat, tethered to a mooring post. After every rain the canoeing counselor—mere me—had to drag it ashore and dump it, or bail and mop it dry.

One night we had a violent storm, and when the before-breakfast dippers went past the canoe dock, someone noted that the old sponson was gone. Its mooring ropes were not too rugged, and they were broken.

Consternation reigned. The State Police were alerted. Some vandal had slipped in under cover of the storm, and stolen that canoe!

The assistant director—another mere man—and I pondered this crime while we breakfasted. It took no Sherlock Holmes to see that a sensible thief would not have taken the worst canoe available, in the most awkward spot for stealing. So it had not been stolen. It had simply sunk.

The lake was murky from the storm, but we swiftly proved our deductions. The never-dry craft had got badly filled with rain. There was a leak in one of the sponsons. The unsinkable craft had sunk. We hauled it out, dried it, patched the sponson, and tethered it again. And we gave thanks that it hadn't filled up when someone was using it. If that had happened, the canoeists would have been helpless, as canoeists. It would have been straight swimming from then on.

All manufacturers will sell you sponson canoes if you want them. They aim to please. E. M. White, master builder that he is, had the grace to try for what have long been called "invisible" sponsons. His models, though really about as invisible as a palomino in a *remuda* of bays, are less awkward than any others I know of.

My emphasis on these dire devices is not too extreme. As soon as you put sponsons on a canoe, you have lost the canoe. Paddling a sponson-equipped canoe is about as sporting as shooting fish in a barrel.

PADDLES

The variations in canoe-paddle shapes throughout the world are almost unbelievable. Paris in his magnificent book (V) shows drawings of dozens, that look like everything from a collegiate initiation stick to an irrigation shovel. It is equally remarkable that, despite the differences in design, they are all used with essentially the same motions.

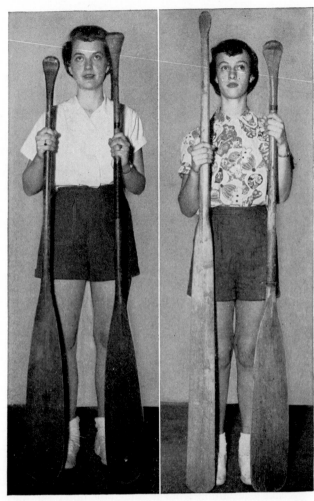

8. Left: Arlene Jones holds a correct length steering paddle (left) and my 1925 Winnetaska model. Right: Sally Bennett compares a Cree paddle (left) with a 66-inch spruce paddle.

Even among the comparatively few Canadian Indian tribes with whom I have worked, there is great variation in paddles. The most extreme are the long, narrow Cree blades, one of which is displayed in the photo by Sally Ann Bennett, who compares it with an average United States model. The Cree paddle is 69½ inches long, with a four-inch blade. The blade is 38 inches long and the shaft only 31 inches.

I argued with the Cree hunters about these paddles. They did not know much English and I knew less Cree, but the paddles themselves spoke a universal language. They liked our factory-made Yankee and Canadian paddles all right—better than their own, it seemed. But they did not change their design. All I saw were identical in shape, but there was some variation in length. Nearly all were longer than the paddlers themselves, for the Crees are a short race. I thought their blades were too narrow, too long, and too thick, their shafts too short and ill-shaped, and their grips too small and too flat. They were all made of spruce, for a very excellent reason. There was nothing else of tree size in that country except some scrubby balsam poplars. My associates, including the frequently quoted Lloyd Melville, who knew the Crees much better than I, did not remotely know why they made paddles as they did. Probably their reasons were fully as valid as those underlying the paleface invention of the straight-arm stroke, or the sponson-created illusion of extra safety. A canoeist trained in the simpler biological sciences swiftly discovers that he is meeting both anthropological and psychological problems quite beyond his ken.

Since everything in the shape of a paddle has been used and used well, the choice of these essential tools must depend on personal opinion, habit, and style. I have managed to use everything I have seen, but my own opinions are definite. There is little basic disagreement among modern white canoeists as to paddles.

For lake paddling I have always liked spruce paddles, and the New England camps for many years strongly favored the Winnetaska models, named for the May Camps. Dr. John B. May was quoted in my old book, as follows:

"My favorite paddle which I used for over ten years, and tried to copy for our camp paddles, was a Canadian Spruce paddle which came just to my nose. The blade is twenty-seven inches long, and the shaft forty inches. The blade is six and a quarter inches wide, though it has lost some by sandpapering in ten seasons. The shaft just above the blade, where the lower hand takes hold, is four and five-eighths inches in circumference, while the only stock paddle I have for measuring is exactly one inch smaller. . . ."

The paddles he describes are just as good now as they were when I worked in his camps in 1923–24.

I told of a very light Winnetaska paddle in my old book. This paddle was bought in the spring of 1925, and I still have it. Though I have not used it in stream paddling, the distances it has pushed canoes are unbelievable. It is 66 inches long; the blade is 26 inches long and 5⅞ inches wide, and the shaft is 40 inches. It is very perfect straight-grained spruce. The dimensions really are ideal for a tall woman's paddle, but men like it just as well.

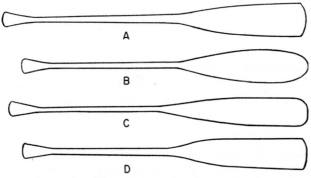

9. Types of paddles. Design is largely a matter of personal preference. B is called a "beavertail," and D is a racing style.

The biggest paddles I ever heard of were unearthed by George Sanborn, Dartmouth '28, in Maine. They were made of ash, were eight feet long, and had blades nine inches wide. I see no reason for using such paddles for canoes.

In general, I have always used the simple rule that a paddle should be three inches under user's height for stern paddling, and six inches under height for bow work—but rarely shorter than five feet and rarely longer than five feet nine inches. Blades should be between five and a half and six and a half inches wide.

Few small children need a paddle shorter than four feet nine inches. I made a paddle small enough for my son when he learned to paddle at the age of six. "Custom" paddles may be needed for odd-sized people.

Any of the standard knob grips do well enough for me, so long as they are smooth. I refuse to suggest hard and fast rules. The paddling rules are rather definite; the rules for paddles are not.

There is general agreement on spruce for lake paddle and racing paddle material, but the average spruce paddle would be kindling wood if used for a mile in tough rapids. In that situation you need hardwood, and many kinds are in use. The most common hardwoods found in commercial paddles are hard maple and white ash. Both are good. Though the maple is smoother, the ash is a little lighter, a little stronger, and less likely to warp. Wild black cherry is also fine paddle material, and at one time was available in commercial paddles. It is the same beautiful cabinet wood that you find in Colonial gate-leg tables and other furniture. It is slightly lighter than either sugar maple or white ash, and not quite as strong as either, but a good piece (all wood is variable) is strong enough.

Black walnut is also beautiful and effective paddle material, especially fine for gift or prize paddles. Paddle walnut should of course be selected from light, straight-grained stock. Contrary to many opinions, walnut is a relatively light-weight hardwood. According to Record (XXI), it averages eight percent lighter than hard maple and four percent lighter than white ash, but three percent heavier than black cherry. Some of the finest, strongest paddles I have ever seen were made of walnut.

A few commercial paddles were formerly made of cucumber wood, which is almost as light as spruce and probably no stronger. It is not rapids material. Douglas fir (Oregon pine) has been used extensively in commercial paddles. It is strong for its weight, and 9 percent lighter than walnut. It is miserably splintery stuff, however, and has no advantages except that it is cheap. If you are unfamiliar with timber and a paddle is called "fir," you had better avoid it.

I have paddled into the thousands of miles with paper birch paddles. I used them because Indians made them from handy material and the price was low. They were excellent too.

In fast water, you entrust your life to your paddle. A broken paddle, even when a spare is handy, can be a very serious matter when traveling in rapids. It compares to broken steering gear in heavy traffic.

The care of paddles is left to the next chapter.

6

The Care of Canoeing Equipment

Since metal canoes have the advantage of needing little care we may dispose of them first. I repeat that aluminum craft need no paint in fresh water. In salt water they do need paint, as recommended by the manufacturer.

Bumps can be beaten out of aluminum hulls with a rubber hammer, and cold aluminum solder for patching is available in any hardware store. A puncture is easily mended with a light canvas patch put on either inside or outside, but more often the former.

Most aluminum canoes today have blocks of Styrofoam—a material which will not absorb water—in the ends rather than air chambers. However, the rubber gaskets must be checked on the air chambers of older aluminum canoes. A leaking gasket could cause a swamped canoe to sink, or at least up-end. The air chambers are of good size, and are ideal for holding small stuff that you want to keep dry—a camera for example. Every time you go out, however, the air-chamber ports should be carefully tightened. Gaskets should be replaced as soon as you note the first sign of oxidation.

Except for the risk of theft or some sort of violence, an aluminum canoe could stay out for years without protection. Common sense, and very little of that, is all that you need to care properly for an aluminum canoe.

All-wood canoes and bark canoes may be ignored here, as most of the readers of this book will never see, to say nothing of use, either of them. Our careful instruction therefore is limited to the far more complicated cedar-and-canvas canoe.

EVERYDAY CARE OF CANVAS CANOES

Good canvas canoes, given good care, may be used for a long time. I owned a Kennebec that was bought in 1916, and was still usable in the late '30's. I gave it away in 1935, when we moved from Park Falls, Wisconsin, to Winona, Minnesota. It was too rickety to be worth moving.

The only canoe I own is now almost exactly sixteen years old. It has been re-covered once, and I would cheerfully risk it in any water that any canoe of comparable size would stand. Barring serious accidents, a well-cared-for canoe could last twenty years or more, even if heavily used. Camps or clubs should figure on writing off canoe values at the rate of 10 percent per year or faster, but individually owned canoes will do far better.

Naturally a canvas canoe should be kept as clean as can be managed, both inside and out. When not in use it should be kept under a roof; or if no roof is available, it should be turned over in the shade and blocked up so that no part touches the ground. Children, for reasons unknown, have a mania for jumping into and onto canoes. This should be drastically prohibited. Cows, peculiarly enough, will also step on canoes when given the opportunity.

Certain camps have rules about always turning canoes over on the racks when not in use. This is quite unnecessary. A canoe that is being used intermittently all day can well sit on a beach right side up, so long as it is dry. Soaking for long periods does damage a canoe. But the inside of a canoe can stand as much sun as the outside if not more. Sun is hard on a paint or varnish finish.

Racks, in the shade if not under a roof, are essential for ordinary beach storage. The canoes should be kept off the ground. The racks should be so located that the canoes will not blow off them, or the canoes should be tied down in heavy winds. In areas where the wind is very violent, such as the north shore of Lake Superior and the east coast of Hudson's Bay, we have frequently piled at least a hundred pounds of rocks on a canoe so that it would not blow away.

Painting

Too much paint is one of the worst enemies of a canvas canoe. My 1933 book advised "light painting."

I have progressed to the point now of advising no paint at all. Varnish the inside at least once a year, the outside as often as three times if you are using the canoe from break-up to freeze-up. My present canoe was re-covered when it was thirteen years old, and it had never been painted after leaving the factory. After re-covering it got three coats of ordinary automobile enamel. Deck paint, thinned 25 percent by spar varnish, would have done as well. It will probably never be painted again as long as I have it.

For painting, if it must be done, various enamels and lacquers are all right, but the cheaper paints listed in the preceding paragraph are good enough. For varnishing, I have found little difference between the best grade of mail-order-house spar varnish and the nationally advertised brands. One lasted as long as the other. I have taken care of as many as 32 canoes belonging to one camp, and the bill of materials for keeping that many in repair is quite appreciable.

I have occasionally scraped and re-finished paint-loaded canoes, first softening the old finish with a blow-torch. This blow-torch work demands some skill, and meticulous care to keep from burning the canvas. You can use paint or varnish remover just as well. Since your canoe should never get paint-loaded in the first place, you are not likely to meet this situation. The procedure is justified, however, as it is cheaper than re-covering, and less work too.

Never put any sort of white lead, linseed oil, or combination of the two on bare canvas. Linseed oil may be the best preservative known for wood, but it oxidizes in cotton fibers. Commercial white lead always has some linseed oil in it, or so I believe. When it has been put on canvas, the material gets weak in a few years and tears like an old slicker. *Never* put white lead on any canvas around your canoe unless the canvas is already so filled that the oil cannot get to the cotton fibers.

Patching

White lead was a universal canoe-patching compound at one time. Even today it is widely recommended. It should never be used at all. I myself did not know any better than to use it until about 1920.

All you need in an ordinary repair kit is a tube or can of fast-drying cement, such as Ambroid or Duco, and a piece of patching cloth. The most suitable fabrics are airplane cloth or balloon "silk"—both made of long-staple Sea Island cotton—though a scrap of heavy nylon cloth is also good. Lacking these in an emergency, use whatever you have; many a piece of shirt sleeve or pants leg has stepped into the breach. A can of marine glue is also desirable in the repair kit. There are several brands. Some have to be used hot.

To patch a small hole, dry the canvas thoroughly with a hot stone or hot axe poll, if you cannot take the time to dry it in the sun. Shave off the paint around the puncture with a jackknife. Cut a patch the size of the shaved area. Smear the spot with cement, smear the patch, press the two together, smear on a little more cement, and dry for five or preferably ten minutes. Of course you will read the cement-maker's directions too.

Repairs made in this way last very well. I have put on "temporary" Ambroid and balloon silk patches that were still on and keeping water out four seasons later. The most experienced Canadian guides I knew were using nothing but a jackknife, "silk," and Ambroid cement by 1930, for both permanent and temporary small repairs. Nothing better has been devised. Even surgeon's tape has lasted for months on a cut canoe.

If you have a real tear, it is better to work a piece of cloth smeared with liquid marine glue under the hole. Stick the cut edges of the canvas down to this, and it is not a bad idea to baste the edges of the seam together with needle and thread. Then stick another piece of cloth over the tear. Thus the inside cloth is glued to the outside cloth, and the whole rupture is pretty well tied together.

If quick-drying cements are not available for small patches, use hot marine glue. It also will dry at once. Some roofing cements are good too, if they are applied hot. The woodsman's stand-by for centuries (I repeat, centuries) was resin or some sort of pitch, slightly softened and toughened with oil or grease. Indians in a past day gathered their own pitch. This is the stuff reported on by Lieutenant Landman (III), and mentioned in Chapter 2. It will melt in the sun, but will last more or less forever if nothing melts it out of a patch or seam.

You can make a fair-enough marine glue from heated commercial resin and a little grease—tallow will do, or lard. You must build a fire, melt it, and smear it on either with or without a patch of cloth. The canvas must be dry, but the melted pitch will harden at once and you can work right along.

Major Operations

If you break planking or ribs, you can improvise repairs by various means, but the only good and permanent way is to take the canoe to pieces and replace the broken parts. Your canoe factory will send you steam-bent ribs, planking, and brass tacks at a moderate price. The factory will also rebuild the canoe, but freight charges as well as repairs are expensive.

To take the canoe apart, you have to remove the stem bands, gunwales, and canvas, so that you can get at the broken parts. You then unclinch and withdraw the nails holding the broken parts, take them out, fit new pieces, nail them in place, and put the works back together.

Certain ingenuity and care are needed in extensive canoe repair, but everything goes along in order when you get at it, and few tools except screw driver, hammer and jackknives are necessary. Two people should work together. This is necessary when clinching tacks. One holds a "dolly bar"—which can be any sort of a chunk of iron—against the piece, and the other drives the tacks against it.

If new ribs do not fit exactly, soak them in very hot water, bend them to shape, and fit them in. The factories steam ribs, but hot water does well enough. White cedar is the most workable wood in the world. Western red cedar is fairly workable.

My Prospector has had a rib or ribs smashed on two occasions. Once it blew off a car as I was unstrapping it on the shore of Lake Bowdoin in Montana. It hit a rock, and a rib was broken in two and planking six inches square was splintered. It did not leak, but eventually it demanded repair. The other time I shot it—of all things—with a ten-gauge shotgun. That time it leaked! But I repaired it instead of hanging it up as a trophy. Freak accident. Few people enjoy the questionable distinction of having shot a canoe.

RE-COVERING CANVAS CANOES

Taking a canoe apart for rib and plank repair is simple, but a lot of work. Re-covering is also a lot of work, and equally simple, but there are some not commonly known devices that will facilitate it.

The canvas comes off a canoe easily after you take out all the screws and rivets in the stem bands and gunwales—carefully, as you'll want to use them again —and loosen the tacks on stems and gunwales. The sheet metal stem band, I repeat, is harder to remove than the conventional bang plate. While you are removing the canvas, the system of fastenings should be noted carefully.

Before the "skin" is off the canoe, or shortly after,

new materials should be assembled. For an ordinary canoe they are as follows:

1. A piece of No. 8 canvas, eight inches to a foot longer than the canoe, and wide enough to go around it, gunwale to gunwale. (Use No. 6 canvas if your canoe is a really big one.)

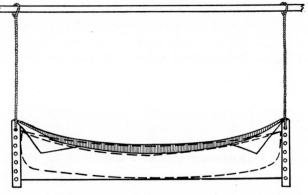

10. Method of re-covering a canvas canoe.

2. Four pieces of two-by-six lumber, of the hardness of Douglas fir or harder, each piece about 30 inches long.

3. A brace and two bits, quarter-inch and three-eighths-inch or half-inch sizes.

4. A dozen or fourteen quarter-inch bolts, about five inches long, with big washers. Square-headed bolts are an advantage.

5. A couple of lengths of quarter-inch rope or clothes line.

6. Wrenches for tightening and loosening nuts.

7. Screw drivers.

8. A couple of hammers. They may well be light.

9. Brass tacks, available from canoe makers if nowhere else.

10. Replacement for any of the old screws or rivets that are imperfect.

11. A pair of pliers, preferably webbing pliers.

12. A sharp knife—an ordinary jackknife is all right.

13. Ten pounds of whiting and one gallon of spar varnish, to make filler. Or get four or five quarts of commercially-made filler if you prefer.

14. A two-inch paint brush for spreading filler.

15. Three pints of canoe enamel, automobile enamel, deck paint, or other hard-finish paint, in the color of your choice.

16. A paint brush or spraying equipment for final painting. The brush mentioned under 14 can do double duty.

17. No. 00 sandpaper.

18. A dry place where the canoe can be hung while the work is going on. A tree limb will do in a dry climate like the West.

You may also need a new keel or new stem bands (bang plates), if the old ones are no longer in usable condition.

The first step is to make a pair of simple clamps, in which to hang canvas and canoe while you work. Each clamp consists of two of the two-by-six pieces, bored with evenly-spaced matched holes to take the quarter-inch bolts. At one end, make a slightly larger hole for the suspension rope. The clamps I now have each consist of one 27-inch and one 30-inch piece, the longer piece bored with a three-eighths-inch rope hole two inches from its end.

Now the simplest procedure is to fold the canvas lengthwise in two, and bolt each end of it into a clamp, forming a sort of hammock. The clamps should be so spaced that the canoe must be pushed down hard to get the stems between them.

When the canoe is in place in the hammock, hang it up and put some weights in it. A hundredweight of stones spread along the keel will be all right. This tends to mold the canvas, and the warmer and drier the weather, the better it will mold. It is a good idea to hang the canoe over night before starting work, but this is not really necessary.

Once everything is ready, begin tacking the canvas to the gunwales. The first two tacks go into the gunwales amidships, one on each side. Then tack away from the middle toward bow and stern, pulling the canvas as taut as possible as each tack is driven. It is a good idea for two people to work together on this, one on each side of the craft.

After tacking has reached within a few inches of both stems on both sides, you take the canoe down and remove the clamps. Then pull one side of the canvas tight across each stem, tack it, and cut it off even with the stem. Next pull the other side of the canvas tight across the first, tack it, and cut it.

The re-covering as such is now finished, and you are ready for filling.

If the canoe manufacturer has sold you some "secret" filler, that is fine. However you can make your own filler quite simply, by mixing ordinary whiting (such as is used to make putty) with equally ordinary spar varnish. Mix them a quart at a time, to the consistency of thick paint. The whiting is very cheap, so you may as well get plenty. I have usually bought it in five-pound packages, and the job on a big canoe has usually bitten into the second package. A gallon of spar varnish is also a logical purchase.

You can spread this mixture well with a paint brush, and rub it in with a scrap of canvas. Let it dry hard. This will take a day in a warm, dry place. You are then ready for painting.

As to paint, canoe enamel, automobile enamel, deck paint cut with 25 percent spar varnish, or any of the hard outdoor paints will be good enough. Brush it on evenly, or spray it if you have the equipment handy. Put on at least two coats, being sure that each is thoroughly dry before the next is applied, and rubbing lightly with sandpaper between them. (No. 00 sandpaper is right for this work.) A third coat of paint is also desirable, and a final coat of spar varnish. Then replace the gunwales, bang plates or stem bands, and keel if any, and the job is done.

A word about fillers: I do not know what ingredients besides those I suggested go into commercial fillers, but I know some of them contain powdered silicon. In other words, powdered sand. Whiting is more like powdered chalk. My filler will last many years, but I think the commercial fillers are slightly better.

A reminder about paints: *Never* put lead or oil paint on bare canvas.

If you want to do a cheap, light re-covering job on an old canoe for occasional use, you can use un-bleached muslin instead of canvas. Stretch on a layer of this; fill it; stretch a second layer over the first while the filler is still wet; and fill that, thus gumming the two layers together. This demands no clamping or hanging. The stuff is stretchy by nature, and shrinks and dries hard after filling. I have re-covered several canoes by this method, and they lasted for years. But naturally the muslin is not nearly so strong as good No. 8 canvas.

Our instruction barge at Idaho State College was made by one of my classes. Its bottom is five-ply Douglas fir veneer, and its sides are pine planks. The outside is canvas-covered and filled, just like a canoe. This craft measures four feet by sixteen feet, and we used it in the swimming pool; anything larger than this would do better in a lake. I once used an instruction barge measuring about six feet by twenty feet. No one argued that this was an unsafe boat for teaching inexperienced paddlers!

PADDLE CARE

Paddle care, though very important, is also very simple.

When paddles are new, it is a good idea to wrap the shafts with cotton trolling line or chalk line. Begin the wrapping about two inches above the blade, and carry it up the shaft for perhaps ten inches. Soak the wrapped area with spar varnish and it will dry hard as bone. The cord is not expensive and the life of the paddle will be doubled, especially if it is spruce.

Lightly sandpaper and varnish softwood paddle blades and shafts at least once a season. If the tips are slightly frayed, really soak them with spar varnish. The grips should not be varnished, but sanded carefully and rubbed with linseed oil. This is solely for hand protection.

Paddles of warpy hardwood, such as maple, will be improved if the unvarnished blades are *soaked* in linseed oil, then well dried and sanded. Quite fine sandpaper, No. 0 or 00, is right for paddle polishing.

Blade checks may be mended with corrugated fasteners, preferably galvanized. They should be driven only half way through the blade, then filed off. The big spruce paddle, companion to the Cree paddle held in the cut by Miss Bennett, had a piece fall out below a corrugated tack. The tack above is still holding. This is still a young paddle—under twenty!— but it will not make very old bones. It is wrapped, but should be wrapped two inches higher.

Paddles should be kept in the shade when not in use, and preferably hanging. To prevent warping, never let wet paddles lie in the sun if it is at all avoidable.

Do not use paddles for horse-play, for crutches, or for other purposes for which they are not intended. On the other hand you do not need to indulge in quite needless paddle worship, as some camps have done. I have heard campers upbraided because they stood with paddles lightly resting on the ground. At this writing I have one paddle that is 28 years old and another three years younger. Both have pushed canoes some thousands of miles, and I have leaned on them when I felt like it—but lightly!

7

Important Canoeing Miscellany

An earlier chapter emphasized a straight lower arm in general paddling, nor was the emphasis too great. In freezing weather, however, when it is very unpleasant to get the lower hand wet—and it will be splashed in ordinary paddling—it is easy and reasonably efficient to paddle with both elbows bent, keeping both hands above the gunwale. I do much of my paddling in this way during the late part of the waterfowl season, when all water is frozen unless it is springy, brackish, fast, or very deep. I use rubber gloves for putting out decoys, but they get ice-caked unless you keep your hands immersed, and it is advantageous to keep your mittens dry if you can.

Further, though it should be a "rule" for young people learning to paddle to stay on their knees, and most good paddlers work in this position in the name of efficiency, it is all right to sit. It is also all right to stand in a canoe when there is reason to do so. This is entirely a matter of balance and judgment.

I have also mentioned that, for practice, you should learn to make a canoe do anything in reason when paddling on one side only. For all that, the canoe has two sides, and there is no reason not to shift when there is occasion to do so. I will not bump a rock because I am too proud to change sides any more than I will fall off a horse because I refuse to grab leather. To prevent my sudden contact with a rough landscape, my saddle horn has been choked until its tongue stuck out.

I knew canoe coaches a generation ago who ruled:

1. Never bend *either* elbow.
2. Never touch the paddle shaft to the gunwale.
3. Never change sides.

These were claimed to be "Indian" rules and principles. They were foisted upon innocent campers who were paying fat fees for sound instruction, and they were exclusively products of the imagination. "Indian" canoeing is no different from Eskimo, Polynesian, or Finnish canoeing. The canoes are different, but the paddles are handled the same way.

RACING

Match racing form is different from that used in cruising. It involves a paddling position on one knee, and it takes years to develop proper balance and muscle control for this. Official racing should be encouraged where the equipment and coaching are available, but it is so time-consuming and expensive that it rates little space in a book on general canoeing. I am ignoring match racing here.

The sort of racing I am here considering is that done while kneeling on both knees in ordinary cruising canoes. Camp, school, and cruising-club racing is the same sort of fun as ranch-horse racing, naval-cutter rowing, or any similar type of standard-equipment competition.

The training that I have had in 'varsity rowing shells, as well as in canoe racing, I have by no means regretted, and I would enjoy experimenting with orthodox racing, given the opportunity. Lacking that opportunity, my racing coaching has been restricted to camp and club racing with ordinary canoes.

An ordinary canoe racing program may be diversified by arbitrary separation into junior, senior, class, or other age and skill groups. You may also have boys', girls', and mixed competition.

Incidentally, I have had fine success teaching girls and women to race. Boys are stronger than girls, but I have trained girls' crews who beat boys' crews in the same age group. In the name of fairness, egotism, or both, I was not coaching the boys that my damsels outclassed!

Though two-way races are out of date in match competition, a race from a starting line around a buoy and back is fine in camp meets. Starting line and buoy should usually be an eighth of a mile apart.

Suggested events are a series of the following:

1. Singles
2. Tandems
3. Fours
4. "War canoe" races, preferably in 20-foot or 22-foot freighters or semi-freighters if war canoes are not available
5. Tail-end race (single paddler kneeling in front of bow seat, paddling alone and without ballast)
6. Standing tandem-paddlers standing on gunwales or seats
7. Crew tilting (dangerous unless equipment is good and supervision is precise)
8. Upset race (get out of canoe, get back in and continue)
9. Double-blade races (if equipment is available)
10. Portaging of various kinds (this is very important, but demands attention and ingenuity)
11. Special events, of value in achieving balance and assisting with life-saving, such as "shaking out" and "splashing out" a canoe; "jouncing"; "gunwale paddling"; and paddling the "figure eight."

In "shaking out," the contestant rolls the canoe over, then turns it right side up, the canoe being completely filled. The craft is then grasped at the stern, the bow tipped up, and the canoe shoved violently forward and back. This shakes most of the water out of it. The canoe is then grasped amidships by the gunwale, and the remaining water is largely "splashed out" by swiftly pumping the gunwale up and down. After this is accomplished, the contestant climbs in over the gunwale without shipping too much water. This takes practice, and swimming instructors just love it. I doubt if it ever saved anyone's life, as anything that would legitimately upset you far from shore would presumably keep you from emptying the canoe. Still it is excellent water practice and hard work, and is highly recommended.

"Jouncing" or "bobbing" consists of standing on a canoe seat or on the gunwales at the stern of the canoe, with no paddle, and urging the canoe forward by violently crouching and rising—like "pumping" a swing as you stand on its seat. By tipping slightly, the canoe can be more or less (frequently less) steered. This too is a water stunt, and contestants frequently fall out.

In "gunwale paddling" you straddle the canoe, a foot on each gunwale, and crouch low enough to paddle. It can be done in singles, tandems, and fours. Contestants frequently fall out or upset while they are getting up onto the gunwales. It is excellent balancing practice, fine for dancers who are learning the split, and like the preceding events hard on cedar-and-canvas canoes because they get water-soaked, softened, and out of shape.

The "figure eight" is real paddling, and the single paddler, without changing sides, actually paddles around this figure in the water. The judge can see this best from a fairly high dock or life-saving tower. The tighter and more symmetrical the figure, the better the record. This requires a clever and swift application of the forward, draw, and push-over strokes, and cannot be done in much of a breeze. It is too easy with two paddlers, but can be done by a lone bow paddler if there is a non-paddling passenger in the stern for ballast. The single-blade contestant paddling in the stern of course does it with no ballast.

WAR CANOES

When my *Elements of Canoeing* was published in 1933, it contained a short chapter on war canoeing. I cannot remotely justify more than a few pages in this book. Though war canoes are still being used, I have not seen one for a good twenty years; and writing as I am in Idaho, I find it hard even to get a good photograph of one.

During seventeen seasons my wife, my son and I, individually or collectively, worked full time for camps —seven different sets of camps, all but one of which had two separate organizations. Three of these groups owned war canoes. Two of them had 25-footers, and one a 35-footer.

I found war canoes useful and a lot of fun. If I were now with a camp that owned one or more, I would use them to the limit. But I would not spend money for them at the cost of getting other canoeing equipment. Twenty-footers rigged like war canoes are now available, and are large enough for most of the things that most people want to do. But a big camp, or a big canoe club, or a college with an extensive aquatic program, could definitely use war canoes, and as definitely profit by their use.

As to handling, war canoes differ little from smaller craft, except that the steersman and the bow man should both be well trained, and the paddlers should be numbered, as in a racing crew. In an outfit as big as this, the words "port" and "starboard" have real meaning. ("Left" and "right" mean the same things, but sound landlubberish.)

11.   Formation paddling at Camp Kehonka, Wolfeboro, New Hampshire.

For all their size, war canoes are easily managed, and can be whirled around with fine speed by good use of the draw and push-over. In this manoeuver, assuming twelve paddlers with the steersman numbered twelve, it is the bow and number two, the steersman and number eleven, who do most of the steering. Three and four, nine and ten help a little; five through eight can scarcely steer at all, though they can help on a pivot.

The steersman of course has to work out proper commands. With any crew, the word to start is "Ready all—hup!" To cease paddling, it is "Let 'er run!" To stop the craft, it is "Hold all!" To execute a turn, it could be "Bow and three, push over. Two and four, draw." Other commands can be worked out easily.

War canoes have had a peculiar history. Dr. John B. May gave me considerable information on their use in racing at about the turn of the century, but so far as I can find out, they haven't been made for this purpose in a long time. They were also very popular for what was called "formal" canoeing. In my first book I quoted some five pages *verbatim* from a paddle-drill article that I still list in the bibliography (XX), but as far as I can discover "formal" canoeing is now a thing of the past.

Still, some campers and some camp directors really loved these canoeing dramatics at one time. I well recall one girls' camp that had three big war canoes, and put on shows with twenty paddlers in each one. These girls had been beautifully coached, but their paddling—well, it reminded me of a conversation I had once with the late James A. Ten Eyck, coach of the Syracuse University crews.

That was shortly before the Intercollegiate Regatta at Poughkeepsie, New York, in 1912; and Stanford University—later a very formidable crew—was making a bid to win the world's greatest rowing classic for the West Coast. I asked the "Old Man" how Stanford was rowing.

"Well," he replied very thoughtfully, "it's this way. They row damned badly, and they do it well."

Like the Stanford crew, these girls paddled in horrible form and did it beautifully. This was no unusual situation in war canoeing thirty-odd years ago, when the straight-arm stroke was in its heyday.

We can dismiss this phase of war canoeing by saying that, if it is ever exhumed, I will not wield the shovel, or the paddle, or whatever excavating tool may be needed. This kind of thing had no more to do with basic canoeing than the manual of arms with shooting, or the goose-step of the German army with route marching. If war canoeing ever enjoys a resurgence of popularity, I trust it will not rejuvenate interest in the straight-arm "J."

DOUBLE-BLADE PADDLING

Double-blade paddling was omitted in the chapter on strokes, because it operates on an entirely different principle from single-blade work. Simply stated, it is forward-facing rowing, the strokes made on alternate sides and without oarlocks.

Double paddles are so rigged that the blades are at right angles to each other. This simplifies feathering. For ease in carrying, they are usually made in two sections, joined by a ferrule at the middle of the shaft when in use. For general-purpose canoeing I prefer them with flat rather than spoon blades. This for the reason that I like to have an extra set of sockets, put grips in them, and use the double blades for a pair of singles when I wish to do so. Single-blade spoons are quite unthinkable! Thus, doubles can be converted to singles and back again in a matter of seconds. By lengthening or shortening the grips, all needed diversity in single-paddle lengths can be obtained—within reason. Still some canoeists prefer spoons, especially for racing.

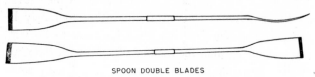

SPOON DOUBLE BLADES

12.   Front and side views of spoon double blades.

Using double blades is—to me—much harder work than paddling with singles, but really experienced double-blade canoeists say that this should not be true. Neither is it true that water must run down the paddle, necessitating drip cups, when the paddle is well handled.

Double-blade paddling is simply dipping—a basic forward stroke—first on one side, then the other. This logically makes for a slight—but very slight—zig-zag to the course. Each stroke is more or less of a sweep, because the blade is operated further away from the canoe than in single-blade forward stroking. You steer or turn by putting more steam on one side and less on the other. Backing, draw, and push-over strokes are the same as with single blades.

Kayaks were designed for double blades, and eight-foot paddles are about right for a good one. If paddles of this length are too large for the kayak you have, I feel that the kayak is narrower than it should be. For a big Guide's Model, a ten-foot double paddle is all right. I used double blades of this sort off and on for several years on the Upper Mississippi Refuge, operating out of Winona, Minnesota. I was frequently alone, and there were instances when I crossed a piece of open water, against the wind, with double blades, when I simply could not have made it with a single blade. When two of us were working a canoe, we rarely took the doubles with us.

You can learn to paddle a kayak with double paddles, and create at least an impression of skill, far faster than you can master the single blade. This is because the very delicate feel necessary in the stern steering stroke is not demanded. Since double-blade paddling is fast and fun, I am all for it. However, it is not popular with most working canoeists, and many a Canadian professional has never touched a double blade, and never will. As I write, I do not own a pair of doubles myself, and have had no occasion to use them—except for demonstration—since leaving the Mississippi in 1940.

All the double-blade paddles I have used were made of spruce, with nickel-plated brass ferrules. These blades all had protecting copper tips. I do not like copper tips on single blades, as I feel that they interfere with smooth manipulation. Double-blade work is comparatively crude, however, when compared with single-blade paddling, and the tips do no harm.

POLING

Poling is, in a way, a finer art than single-blade paddling. It is rather neglected in this country, though "punting" with a pole is common in England.

Landman (III) mentions his canoemen carrying "a ten foot setting pole, of good ash, and shod with an iron ferrule at each end." We will agree with him as to pole length, but prefer smooth spruce to ash; and we find a steel socket on one end good enough for all the poling most of us will ever do. Those old freighters sometimes used the two-ferrule poles like double blades.

13. Patricia Lavens Jones compares a duck-bill (lower) and setting pole (top).

The two pole tips held by Pat Jones in the cut are typical setting-pole and duck-bill models. The duck-bill of course is for mud, and a nine-foot pole is long enough for this. But I have seen New Brunswick polers on the Tobique, Nipisiguit, and Upsalquitch Rivers use spruce poles as long as twelve feet, and these polers were *very* skilled men.

Any blacksmith can make the setting tips. They are about seven inches long, and the pole sockets are one and a half inches in diameter. The one in the photograph is the last of five that I bought from the Chestnut Canoe Company of Fredericton, New Brunswick, in 1924. The only United States canoe company from whom I have bought them—or poles either—is White of Old Town, Maine, though others may sell them. White's poles also were of "good ash."

Duck-bill sockets were formerly made in Minneapolis, but are said not to be available at this time. The ferrule for the pole on the one shown is only one and a quarter inches in diameter, and not much more than that in depth. I think the socket should be one and a half inches across, and at least two inches deep. A spruce pole tends to work loose. This duck-bill pole has at times been invaluable in marsh duck-hunting.

All poles should be carefully sandpapered, and well treated with linseed oil. Soak in all the oil they will take, dry, and sand again.

Moore (XV) describes a tube-type pole tip that will hold better on smooth rocks than an ordinary steel tip. He gives excellent advice on poling, but I do not agree that one should never change sides.

A description of poling is not easy, and poling upstream, as it is usually done, is *very* hard work. You can usually paddle down the stream that you must go up with a pole.

Though paddling is quite sexless, poling is only for men or very carefully trained women. I have never seen a white woman who was a good poler, though I know no reason why skin color alone should be a drawback.

For easy poling upstream in fast water, it is advantageous to have a canoe 18 feet long or longer. You definitely do not want a keel on a poled canoe, except possibly a flat one for protection only.

Poling is done standing, in such a position that the canoe balances with the bow slightly clearing the water. This needs practice. Sometimes, with a heavy load and a big canoe, the bow man may use a short pole from his knees. But in general, with an ordinary load (one passenger or a couple of hundred pounds of freight) the poler goes it alone.

In theory, poling is very simple. You drop the pole tip to the bottom, give a shove, recover, and do the same thing over again. Actually, a pole operates much the same as a paddle, and anyone can get to be a fair enough poler through experimental practice. You may fall out occasionally, but the water is reasonably shallow or you could not pole.

In practice, form is important. To describe the simplest and best form, let us assume that the poler is working on the left side of the canoe and shoving upstream, in water not over two feet deep.

The first step is to grasp the pole with the left hand, the pole resting on the bottom and pointing slightly backward, while the hand is at about the height of the poler's hip. The right hand grasps the pole at a convenient height above the left. Now the pole is thrust back—hard—the body going into a crouch. The canoe glides forward.

To recover, the poler straightens and lifts his left arm without changing the point of grasp of either hand. He then swings his right hand down, perhaps a couple of feet below the upflung left hand, and lightly guides the pole forward. At a convenient spot in the forward glide of the canoe, the pole is again dropped to the bottom, the right hand is swung up, and the thrust is repeated.

We repeat that, if the water is shallow—as it often is —the hand toward the side on which one is poling stays at about the same spot on the pole. If the water is deep, you may have to "climb" the pole to some extent, and toss the pole up for the next stroke. I had some tough training in deep water, and got so this pole tossing is rather habitual. The overhand stroke, however, is most efficient when it is mastered.

In very shallow, rough streams you may snub down with a pole. You have the advantage of being able to come to a full stop, even in fast water, by snubbing the canoe, hard, first on one side, then on the other.

With the pole on the bottom in the course of the stroke, you guide the canoe by pulling the pole tip toward it or shoving away. Great care must be taken to keep the keel (bottom of the canoe where a keel might be) in line with the current, except in the immediate act of turning. An actual deep keel is grabbed by the current, and is more embarrassing when poling than when paddling in fast water.

There is no human motion anywhere, in sport or art, that shows a finer combination of grace and power than the work of a good poler.

GENERAL INFORMATION

Stroke Speeds

In my old book Dr. May was quoted as saying that northern woodsmen average 45 strokes a minute. My observation, during the very few times I have checked speed, is in agreement. Dr. May also mentioned paddlers doing 90 strokes a minute at the end of a war canoe race.

Conditions, the height of the paddler, and the length of the paddle, to say nothing of style, will all make sharp differences in stroking speed. Probably about 30 strokes a minute is as slow as any trained paddler will work. The "paddle trailer" may be ignored in this connection.

Cruising Distances

Cruising distances, like stroke speed, vary with conditions. I doubt if professional Canadian canoeists, using more-or-less loaded canoes week after week, average over 15 miles a day or perhaps a hundred miles a week.

My old book reported a trip that I took with two companions, on which we did 70 miles down stream, including two short portages, in a 14-hour day. In dead water, with one assistant and about 200 pounds of freight, I have several times paddled a distance of 35 miles in a rather long day.

A big party congests portages and slows time. I was once on a 17-day trip with 11 canoes. Someone had to act as traffic officer until we got a real travel and portage plan developed. This same party covered about 50 miles down stream in one day on the Mississauga River in the Algoma District of Ontario. Some of the water was very fast, and there were several portages.

Towing

The dangers of towing were carefully explained in the section on safety. Still canoes must frequently be towed; and in that case a "bridle" must be used as shown in the illustration. If you tow a string of canoes, there must be a bridle at each end of each one.

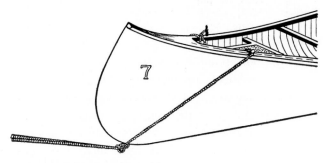

14. A form of towing bridle.

For multiple towing, medium sized canoes may be lashed together in catamaran or pontoon style. Some experimenting must be done to get them the right distance apart if they are lashed together with poles, and the lengths of the towing ropes are also dependent upon various factors of engine speed, wind, and load. We have thus towed two "teams" of canoes with a forward "team" propelled by an outboard motor, six in all being moved by the one engine. The engine has the advantage of not getting tired.

Canoes lashed together in "teams," with poles tied across the thwarts and diagonal brace poles, will not upset. But again note that any properly handled canoe will not upset in water where it may legitimately be used. That does not mean that it will not swamp.

Kneeling Cushions

An Indian may kneel all day on cedar ribs and not mind it. If he does mind it, he does not say or do anything about it. Admirable in some ways perhaps, but foolish, though I admit you can get used to kneeling on bare boards.

You need knee pads. If you are on a long trip you improvise something.

Sponge rubber pads clipped to the knees with surgical elastic are light and permanent, and will not get lost if you wear them just as regularly as your boots. Pneumatic cushions are not bad, but they can puncture. Shaved or ground cork, such as Spanish grapes are packed in, makes good knee pads, if put in slim cushions about two feet long. They also double as life preservers.

CARRYING

Portaging canoes on a truck, car, or wagon needs simple ingenuity. All sorts of patent and quickly removable boat and baggage racks are available for cars.

15. A 16-foot Prospector canoe on top of ¾ ton pickup truck.

I have lugged canoes on them for some thousands of miles, always expecting the craft to blow off. I do not trust a canoe on any of them.

An illustration shows my 16-foot Prospector on my 1953 three-quarter-ton pickup truck. The canoe is just long enough to fit there; if it were longer, it would have to be shoved well forward so as not to interfere with a trailer. I frequently lug a canoe on a truck, and drag a horse or two in a trailer behind it.

It is easy to rig a two-canoe trailer on an axle. One canoe should be above the other, and both should be carried right side up. It is equally easy to make racks that will carry half a dozen canoes on a big stake-body truck. But large-scale hauling needs pre-season preparation and the special attention of skilled mechanics. Padded cradles must be made to fit each individual canoe, and loading them is a considerable chore.

In all instances, padding must be perfect, as nothing —not even a crack-up in rapids—is as likely to damage a canoe as improper hauling.

However a one-canoe or one-boat rack, bolted on a car top, permits you to slap a canoe on top of a car —alone—and strap it down in a couple of minutes. I have taken mine off in one minute.

My rig consists of two brackets, of which the rear one is a piece of pipe with a length of heavy rubber hose on it, both rolling around a steel shaft that is welded to uprights of ordinary one-and-a-half-inch black steel pipe. You tilt the canoe against the roller, and then roll it forward as far as you wish. The hose should be of high quality and not less than one inch inside diameter.

To attach this to an ordinary car (an all-steel-top station wagon or carry-all is best) you have a piece of four-by-four cut to fit the top. You fasten this in place with bolts through the top, and you rig it with iron bearings so the roller will operate. Rings may be welded to the bolts.

The front bracket is simply another fitted four-by-four, rubber padded, and equipped with either ring bolts or eye bolts.

Properly installed, this device will neither move nor leak. Such a combination of canoe, tent-pole, and general carrying rack should be available for station wagons as standard extra equipment, but I have not seen any.

I use friction buckles, strong one-and-a-half-inch web straps, and big galvanized snaps to hold the canoe down to the rack. If the straps are kept dry you can draw them rather tight, and they will not let the load shift. The secret of safe car portaging is to let nothing budge. At times, during some 14 years as a federal biologist, I carried a canoe on my car as regularly as I carried a pair of binoculars. I know that I have thus carried canoes over 50,000 miles, and I tried all manner of fastenings before finally concentrating on the rubber roller and web straps.

If ingenuity is the prime requisite for wagon or car portaging, a comfortable (?) yoke, a strong back, and a weak mind are all important when the canoe must be lugged by human jackass power.

Of course canoe portaging is just one form of portaging, and lugging packs was ancient business when Xerxes invaded Greece. A canoe is one of the meaner things to lug. Not as mean as a kitchen stove or a piano, but mean. In 1914 I first heard the idea that if you packed so much that your ears lengthened an inch, it was time to lay off and let them shrink. My ears have been stretched to such asinine length and my backbone shortened by so many dire loads that I discuss this subject with most intense emotion. However, my mental status still permits me to lug a canoe, a quarter of moose meat, and other equally heavy and awkward objects. With a sounder mind, I would have either managed to have someone else do the lugging, or graduated to pipe and slippers.

My reference to mental status and packing is not intended solely as an effort to be funny. One of the most important values of the canoe is that it is the most portable really good boat that exists. If you cannot carry it, you have passed up this value. And I repeat that packing is largely a state of mind. Whether that state is weak or strong may be open to argument. Its other psychological peculiarities are *definite* enough.

From the mental viewpoint, packing anything is like ignoring the kick of a gun, running long distances, or rolling with the blow of a boxing glove. It takes an admitted minimum of muscle to wind a 90-pound canoe around your neck and trot over a portage, but it is twice as easy if you know that you can do it and decide that you are going to do it. A sound person will not be injured by lugging a canoe. If you are not sound there is no surer way to discover it!

My minimum requirements for a camp canoeing counselor, if a man, are listed in a later chapter to include carrying a 65-pound canoe half a mile in not over fifteen minutes. No canoe weighing less than 65 pounds is fit for general use, and the time stated is not fast. I have carried an 85-pound canoe a mile in twenty minutes, admitting that I had reason to hurry!

My requirements do not include the portaging of canoes by boys, under sixteen, or by women of any age. For all that, in one camp, I had an Ann Arbor boy named "Corky" Cortright who was only fourteen, and who could go over a portage on the dog-trot with an 85-pound canoe. In the same camp a sixteen-year-old from Cleveland, named Harold ("Snow") North, could carry his weight (140 pounds) over a mile portage without a rest, and finish apparently as fresh as a daisy. Nearly all boys can learn to pack.

I have had excellent success teaching girls and women ordinary packing and portaging. My wife has occasionally carried as much as 85 pounds on a portage, and I have known a number of run-of-the-mill women who could do likewise. I make no reference to upper Canadian Indian women, who ask no packing odds from the men.

However, in canoe portaging, balance is so important and ankle and knee strain so great that I have been squeamish about teaching females to lug canoes. Studies of camp injuries through long periods proved that boys got generally messed up far more than girls, but that the damsels were more likely to injure ankles, and much more likely to injure knees. If you go down under a canoe, a knee is very likely to get it.

You will note a picture of Pat Jones, one of my 1953 Camp Class students, lugging a canoe. It weighs about

16. Patricia Lavens Jones lugs a 90-pound canoe with a hewn yoke bolted in the place of the middle thwart.

90 pounds, including the yoke and a paddle. She did not carry it far, but anyone would be foolish to wager that she could not carry it half a mile with a month's training. She stands about five feet eight, and even if she were not a Marine's wife she would be no soft wolf bait. However, not many women, even the most modern and emancipated, will be able to carry a canoe alone without paying too big a price. Two can carry one easily, and four more easily still.

Most ordinary canoes that weigh not much over a hundred pounds can be carried well enough by one man, and carried considerable distances. When I was young and agile, I worked one eight-mile portage, but there are very few longer than three miles. The great majority range from a mere "lift over" to perhaps a mile and a quarter.

The most important help in carrying a canoe is the carrying rig. My yoke, bolted in to replace the Prospector's middle thwart, is clear enough in the cuts. It is hand whittled from a slab of basswood, and I have another made of black ash. Any medium-light but tough hardwood will do. This yoke is made to fit my shoulders, but no one seems to have trouble using it. Various shapes are possible. You might study museum specimens of milk-maids' yokes and sap-carrying yokes, if you have not been where they still use them.

You will also note the leather tump line in the photo of Mrs. Jones. She is easing the tump line with her hands, as an authentic *voyageur* should, and balancing the canoe with her elbows under the gunwales. If her hands were not on the tump straps, they should be forward, with fingers hooked under the gunwales. Of course everyone will develop his own carrying style through experience.

The great advantage of the combination shown is that you can tighten, loosen, or remove the tump line, and ease certain muscles. Tump-line packing does not

17. Close-up of carrying yoke and head-line.

favor the swan neck. I am just about average size as I write (five feet nine, 160 pounds), but a dozen pounds heavier than when I first started working in the woods. I have long worn a size 16 collar, however, and I am now much happier if it is size 16½ (and not buttoned!). At least an inch of that contribution from the haberdasher can be charged to the tump line. I do not know that a muscular neck has ever been a disadvantage to any man.

There are various kinds of detachable yokes; I have

often improvised them from paddles. I say much, however, for the permanently bolted-in yoke. You cannot lose it, and there is no excuse for not making your own except indolence. A three-foot slab of light hardwood should be easy to come by. You bolt the yoke in just like a thwart, placing it just forward of the canoe's horizontal center of gravity—i.e., so that the craft tips back a little when it is carried. If you don't get it just right, you can add a little weight fore or aft. My canoe balances best with a paddle back in the stern.

There are various methods of picking up a canoe. The most elementary is to roll the canoe over so that one end rests on something several feet off the ground, and then stoop under it. In the woods this is considered a "sissy" method.

The easiest method I know of is for the packer to pick up the canoe by its middle, and have it sit on his "lap" as he stands in a slight crouch. If he is right-handed the bow should be to his right, and the long axis of the yoke should point to his left hip bone. His right hand holds the far gunwale, and his left hand the near gunwale.

To get the canoe up, he gives a hard boost with his left knee, drops his left hand from the gunwale, crooks his left arm (at the elbow) under the gunwale at about the point from which he dropped the left hand, and rolls the canoe over his head with the leverage of the left biceps and deltoid. The yoke should settle around his neck.

This motion is quick. Any hesitancy and you are

undone. Many do it right the first time, and correctly ever after. Little strength is demanded if the form is right.

As to personal portaging, my final advice is this: After you have learned all about it, turn the job over to someone else. That is, if you are smart. My oft-quoted guide friend, Lloyd Melville, told the best story I ever heard about a smart camp counselor.

Melville met this fellow on a long carry in the Algoma District of Ontario—a rugged young man, marching at the head of a line of boys lugging canoes and packs. He was playing a lively air on a harmonica, but was carrying nothing else. Explained to Lloyd that the boys packed better if they had a little martial music.

UPSTREAM PADDLING

There are many places where the water is too deep to pole, or where poling is impracticable, yet you can do fine bucking the current with a paddle. The Colorado River, below Hoover Dam, has the worst current my wife and I ever attempted to buck. Fishing in that area, we occasionally worked upstream with the canoe. A mile an hour was faster time than we ever made, but we were able to gain on the shallow side of the current.

Moore (XV) gives excellent advice on upstream work. Everyone agrees that, on a crooked stream, you stick to the *inside* of each curve, cut each point closely, and then work into the inside of the next curve. In going upstream you simply study the current and paddle where it is slowest. You sneak into eddies, save your power when you can, and lean on like mad when you must. Upstream work demands a strong paddle.

Poling has already been discussed, but where poling is insufficient and paddling impossible, you may be able to track (tow) a canoe through fast water with a Y-line, attached stern and bow. If the Y-line is correctly proportioned, the bow will stay off shore. The "Y" is so built that the pull on the line attached at or near the stern is a little stronger than the pull on the bow. The bow is thus kept out into the current because the stern is angled slightly toward shore. It takes a little juggling to get this right, so I hesitate either to use a diagram or suggest actual rope lengths. The speed of the current, size of the canoe, and balance and weight of the load will all have to be coordinated with the tracking lines. You rarely need this device in ordinary paddling, but when you do it may save a lot of portaging.

Lieutenant Landman's (III) "Hambro lines" were primarily for tracking. I have an idea that about six of that freight crew towed and four stayed aboard to steer and pole. In a party of two, one can sometimes stay on board and pole while the other tracks. Sometimes both track.

In shallow water you can pole with a hardwood paddle, using it edgewise. I have seen six-and-a-half-foot paddles made for combination poling, and big bateaux (pointer) paddles rigged with spiked steel tips. These are the genuine Paul-Bunyan-size paddling tools that definitely separate the men from the boys, or the girls either unless they are Amazons.

In upstream paddle-poling the steersman—in a crew of two—furnishes most of the power and the bow man does most of the steering.

LOADING

Proper loading of a canoe cannot be over-emphasized. Much must be learned by experience, but there are some rules as definite as mathematical axioms.

The first rule is: *Do not overload.* What is safe in certain types of water is dangerous in others. I have ferried six fully-grown people across a deep creek in my 16-foot Prospector. This craft leaves four inches of freeboard when loaded with 850 pounds, which is not enough freeboard except in very calm weather. I had at least 950 pounds in it during this ferrying, and too much weight was above the gunwales. We managed, of course, but one must specifically know his limitations.

We are frequently asked what weight is safe in a canoe in ordinary cruising. The size of the canoe has a lot to do with the answer.

In such models as my 16-foot Prospector, the Chestnut 18-foot Cruiser, or the White 18½-foot Guide's Special Model, I would not trust a load of over 600 pounds, including crew, on an average trip. Some 300 pounds of crew and 300 pounds of freight would be plenty. Nor would I take a long trip in canoes smaller than those specified. Many do, and get away with it. More power to them.

The 20-foot Guide's Special canoes will handle half a ton in any water within reason. Paddling is easiest with a crew of either two or four. Some camps have erred in making trips with canoes that were too small. I have seen three people riding in small 16-foot canoes, one sitting as a passenger twiddling his thumbs. Everyone should paddle, even if the number is odd. Four people, including camping equipment, can take trips in a 20-footer.

The load must be kept as low as possible, simply to insure a low center of gravity. It is perhaps trite to say that the load should be balanced so that the canoe will not list. But I have been in canoes with people who were utterly unconscious of list, and apparently had no sense of balance or even a mild interest in it. These, though rare, are the ones who make canoeists turn gray.

For lake paddling, load the bow heavily when working into the wind. A fattish damsel, who incidentally paddles well, makes an ideal bow decoration when battling a brisk breeze. But too heavy a bow will make the canoe wallow and ship water in very heavy seas. It may then be time to get ashore, bail, pray, or combine all known salvaging principles. When going with the wind the bow should be light, but the stern should not be so low that waves will come in over it. This is always an indication that you would be better off on shore. I have occasionally kept a canoe afloat by bailing. It is embarrassing, but I am still alive.

On swift water, going either upstream or down with little wind, I like my bow light. This is especially important in poling. A combination of fast water and heavy wind always adds up to grief. Going down a fast current against a heavy wind is the most dangerous kind of canoeing one is likely to find. It is worse if the sun is in your eyes.

If a canoe is loaded with heavier-than-water freight, the stuff should be so arranged that it can be pitched out in an emergency. Sinking is the last thing in the world that should happen to a canoe. It may be the last thing that *will* happen to it! I have lugged a few cargoes of fossil bones along the shore of American Falls Reservoir in Idaho. Fossil elephant bones are as sinky a freight as I have ever handled, and I had to be very cagey on this assignment. I have never yet had to jettison heavy cargo, but in several instances I came so close to it that perhaps I lost some hair, and what remained lost some color.

The distribution of human freight is also important. This should be obvious, but some folks can't see it. Nothing is more pitifully humorous than a green paddler, alone in a canoe, sitting on the stern seat and trying to paddle against the wind. It should not be necessary to dwell on this, but I have seen strong, intelligent men, educated up to the doctorate, trying to do this in defiance of all physical laws. The manufacturer had put a stern seat in the canoe, so the victim figured he had to sit on it, with or without ballast.

Earlier we have mentioned that, in bucking a wind, the canoe has to go more or less down hill. If you are paddling alone, you must crawl forward until this down-hill balance is accomplished. You can then paddle away. But of course there are winds that cannot be bucked by any single paddler, or any crew either. You have to know when to stay ashore, or get ashore if you can.

I am sometimes asked whether it pays for a lone single-blade paddler to tip a canoe up on the bilge, and paddle it continuously tipped. I have so rarely had occasion to paddle an unloaded canoe single blade, alone, that the question is rather academic. I have seen canoeists of the "smart alec" type paddle this way so much that I am prejudiced against it, but the prejudice may not be justified. Claussen (VI) favors it, with strict limitations, in a wide canoe. If you kneel the position is not dangerous. It may be dismissed as relatively unimportant, and at least partially a stunt.

Canoeing duffel must first of all be as light, as compact, and as waterproof as possible. Pine boxes are fine for carrying food. They should be made to fit the canoe, and are best if rigged with hinged tops and rope handles. Some like temporary boxes to throw away when empty, others like permanent containers that must be lugged home. Pack baskets have their points, and so do ordinary packs, with boards so that tin cans will not gouge the portagers' backs.

I have known expert Canadians who would not put a box in a canoe. Others use nothing else for food. But food containers, as well as everything else carried in a canoe, are more properly technical camping problems than technical canoeing problems.

In paddling under risky conditions, valuable heavy tools, like guns, should be tied down. I repeat I have never had a canoe fill in deep water. But I have tied things fast many times, and in the meantime have done my best to get to shore. In such situations it is well to heed the Shakespearean dictum:

> "Stand not upon the order of your going,
> But go at once."

CANOEING ETIQUETTE

Woodsmen (especially Canadians) and cow hands are the most polite people I have ever known. Good manners admittedly follow a slightly different code on the river than they do in the drawing room. But basic politeness, which is consideration for the other fellow first, can never be mistaken anywhere. A veneer of good form is quite different.

There are old, established customs for canoeists that of course are slipping, but it is desirable to observe them.

It is bad form for one flotilla of canoes to pass another going the same way, unless the first one stops and lets it by. Unless a guide knows the water extremely well, rushing by is dangerous as well as discourteous on a river. You may run into bad water.

If you are catching up with another party, stay well back of them unless they stop. If they know what they should do, they will either speed up and get out of your way, or halt and let you go by. There should always be a few words of greeting between leaders. It is a very good idea to know who is who, and where he is going. Tell them—roughly—your own plans. If they do not reciprocate, you have at least done your duty.

Wherever they are going, or whatever their method of transportation—excepting cars we suppose—back-country travelers should always stop to "pass the time of day" when they meet. If they are far enough back, cars too should stop.

It is never a good plan to hurry on a river trip. *Voyageurs* must sometimes go incredible distances in very short periods. Still they are never in too great a hurry to stop and say "hello." They always get up early, and they may travel late, but they make haste slowly.

French Canadians of a past generation, even if they knew each other well and had no occasion to talk, always rested their paddles across the gunwales and let their canoes *drift* by each other when they met. The accepted salutation was "Quay, quay." I was never sure of the spelling, and no one was ever able to tell me precisely what it meant, but it was the proper thing to say. You slowed down too, and if the other chap had any questions, you were not going too fast to answer them.

It has always been bad form to appropriate a camp site regularly used by any other party, when the other party planned to use it. On certain much-traveled canoe routes, there have been races for certain good camp sites for many years. This may be unavoidable, but it is certainly lamentable.

Discourtesies have been mounting, largely as a result of too much gasoline. They should be kept down on the canoe routes. The fact that the other party is discourteous is no excuse for you to follow their example.

Probably the saddest discourtesies met today are the patronizing if not sneering attitudes put on by tourists in contact with "natives." It is poor form, of course, to refer to anyone as a "native," unless you do so in exactly the right tone of voice and with the proper smile. If you chance to have read Owen Wister's *The Virginian,* you will remember that you can call anyone almost anything, if you smile! I have ridden over Mount Wister, near the Idaho-Montana-Wyoming corner, and the whole country is still rough enough to demand courtesy to the environment.

In much of the finest canoe country of New England, New York, and the Lake States, more and more water frontage is being bought up by more and more people who do not favor camping on their shores. Discourteous water parties, like discourteous hunters, have become so rough that some people will not tolerate *any* campers. This is a cross that must be carried. But frequently proper contacts in advance will make carefully-conducted canoe parties not only tolerated but welcome. There have been occasions when people who at first wanted my parties to move on ended by giving us a gallon of milk, a dozen eggs, a watermelon, and an invitation to camp any time we passed.

I do not like to camp where there is anyone else around, but this is sometimes unavoidable, and will be more unavoidable as population increases. Fortunately the National Forests are holding their own, and State and other public lands are gaining. This may have little to do with basic canoeing courtesy, but let me assure you that the Forest Service and State forest employees are some more people you had better respect. They are the canoe camper's best friends.

In addition to certain courtesies between the canoeing party and the public, discipline, which is a form of courtesy, is most important within the party itself.

In many cases canoes should be bunched; in others, well spread out. The leader, if he is competent, knows what is safe. If he is not competent he has no business to be the leader, and someone has blundered. Big parties possibly should travel in two or even three waves, so that small landings and narrow portages will not be congested. On our big trips in Canada the head guide always led. Someone (usually me) had to be in the clean-up spot. Our trailing canoes were sometimes a mile behind the leaders. The guide was the dictator.

Many young people who go to the woods have not been subected to very rigid discipline. The canoe forces discipline through the environment, and the environment can be harsh if you do not understand it or refuse to cooperate with it. Breaches in canoeing discipline have many times been punished by death.

CANOE-TRIP SHELTERS

This is no camping textbook, and I have a foot-high stack of notes and past writings that may easily become one before many snows melt. But I am frequently asked questions about "sleeping under a canoe," and here discuss it by demand rather than choice.

In the East and the Lake States, summer rains are so frequent that canoe trips without tents are indeed foolish. Many camps for which I worked used to take trips without tents. This was originally due to the cupidity of the camp owners, but they provided tents for my trips as soon as I really went on the war path. Some of them had tents of the finest type before I entered their employ. Some did not have anything. The campers improvised poncho or tarpaulin shelters when it rained, but were more or less miserable.

In the West, you can generally get along without a tent by August or even earlier in the season. Around the high lakes, such as those in Yellowstone National Park and Glacier National Park, it does not rain often. But when it rains—brother, how it rains!

A big canoe tipped on its side, with a light tarp drawn over it to make a sort of lean-to, will sleep a couple of people—all that should be travelling in such a canoe—well enough.

A very light tent for two people can be had in a weight of under seven pounds, and still be durable, comfortable, and absolutely waterproof. It is a pious idea to get one, if you can, and store other supplies under the canoe. I have taken canoe trips without a tent because I lacked both the tent and the where- withal for purchasing one. I had a canoe, and that was about all. Circumstances alter cases, and nowadays simple camping equipment is a small part of the budget for people who can afford to get to where the canoeing starts.

To those starting on a shoestring, a scrap of canvas pulled over the eaves of an up-turned canoe may be a palace.

8

Canoe Sailing

When *The Elements of Canoeing* was published in 1933, I borrowed all the sailing information. It was written by Waldemar Van Brunt Claussen, and copied by permission from the 1931 edition of *Canoeing*, published by the Boy Scouts of America.

I knew little about sailing in 1933, and have not learned much since. Mr. Claussen was an expert sailor when he wrote the 1931 account, and still is. However I cannot find that he or anyone else has written anything about canoe sailing that is as authoritative as these instructions, so they are reproduced as they were. They are much more complete than the sailing information in the 1952 Scout Manual.

I might add that nylon is now known as a fine, light cloth for sails. As to leeboard material, Philippine mahogany is suggested. It is now rather readily available.

Perhaps I should stress that sailing a canoe is not essentially different from sailing any other small boat. At one time sailing canoes, so called, were made with

18. Standard commercial sailing rig in action.

centerboards. I saw them in use in New York not far from the turn of the century. There doubtless are some in American Canoe Association boathouses that are still being used. However few who read this will ever see one, to say nothing of using one, unless there is a rejuvenation of interest in specialty canoeing. This is of course possible.

Improvised sails, though tricky, have been used with
value and safety. If a canoe is big and you do not
try to sail into the wind, you can get by without leeboards.

So far as I could see, the salt-water Cree and
Eskimo sailors of Hudson's Bay did not use leeboards,
but a squaw or papoose frequently would hold a
paddle in lieu of a leeboard over the side of the canoe.
Those long, lean blades really went down and held.

19. Cree Indians of James Bay, Canada, sail their canoes
on the way to the goose marshes.

The rigs would not suggest that the Crees were very
good sailors. The sails, in the shape of triangles wrong
side up, were peculiar. The cut shows more than I can
describe. They got along, however, frequently lugging
everything that they owned in a canoe, travelling hundreds of miles, and sometimes cutting across big bays
so that they were miles from shore. Their smallest

canoes were 18-foot freighters, with about 46-inch beam, 18-inch depth, and three-quarter-ton capacity. Some were much larger, with ton-and-a-half capacity. The wrong-side-up sails were invariable.

Though the Hudson's Bay natives are of course non-swimmers, sailors using the light rigs described below had better count on an occasional ducking. I clearly emphasized in Chapter 3 that a good canoeist could paddle all of his life (and a long life) without ever swimming. I have never known a canoe sailor who did not upset rather frequently. I do not know enough about sailing to state whether or not sailing upsets can be prevented. Since there is no law against them, you had better prepare to swim.

Mr. Claussen's notes follow: °

MAKING THE "RIG"

Regular "store" rigs are faulty in many respects. The sails are usually poorly cut and of inferior materials. Masts are so tall that they are dangerous on account of raising the center of pressure too high. Spars are poorly made. Leeboards of the usual type are absolutely useless for windward work, as they do not extend sufficiently below the keel to offer a proper purchase on the water. Most canoes are rigged without regard to proper balance and therefore will not sail well to windward and are difficult to handle at all times.

° Reprinted with the permission of the Boy Scouts of America from *Canoeing*, 1931.

The sail should be made of fine Egyptian cotton, 3-ounce No. 1 sail cloth, or balloon silk, and should be cut rather full on the gaff and boom, and with a well rounded leach. This rounded leach is held out with three light battens slipped into pockets. For

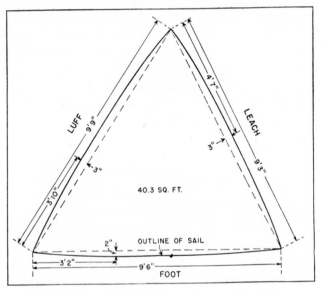

LUFF 9'9"

LEACH

4'7"

3"

3"

9'3"

3'10"

40.3 SQ. FT.

2"   OUTLINE OF SAIL

3'2"   9'6"

FOOT

20. Sail for a 17-foot canoe.

battens it has been found that the best wood comes from the thin sides of an ordinary egg crate; it is pliable and tough without much weight. Seams in the sail should run as indicated; edges along the gaff and boom should be strongly reinforced with non-stretching sailmakers' tape. For a 17-foot model, a good

conservative size would be 40 square feet—this would
be about 9 feet 6 inches along each spar and 9 feet
3 inches along the leach. The fullness on the gaff and
boom is obtained by cutting these edges of the sail
slightly convex instead of straight.

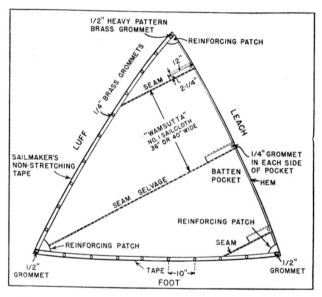

21.　Pattern for a sail.

The sail may have regular brass grommets along two
edges for lacing to the spars, but better results are
obtained with small galvanized or brass rings along
the edges of the sail. Screw small brass screw-eyes
along the gaff and boom, spacing them exactly half-
way between the rings on the sail, and then lace a

strong piece of well waxed cod line, or fine phosphor bronze braided wire through the rings and eyes, and fasten it at one end with a small screw into the spar, and at the other end with a small brass turn-buckle. The ends of the sails are then drawn out and fastened with a rawhide thong to the ends of the spars. With this arrangement it is possible to slack off the sail each time it is put away, or accidentally wetted and it will not be pulled out of shape even through years of use.

The gaff and the boom should be clear straight-grained spruce about 11 feet long (they can *later* be trimmed to fit the sail more comfortably), and 1½ inches at the middle, tapering to ⅝ inch at the ends. These spars are joined with a piece of heavy rawhide with a long brass screw and washer. Drill the ends of the spar before inserting the screws, so that there is no danger of splitting. The rawhide makes a good steady joint, but a joint consisting of brass screw-eyes and an S-hook may also be used. The brass jaw (for holding the boom close to the mast) is best made of ⅜-inch half-round brass bent as indicated; fasten this to the boom with two small screws located as shown in the sketch, and then serve tightly with chalk-line or fish-line and give a finishing coat of shellac. Do not get a screw hole near the bend or the jaw will break there under heavy strain; depend on the serving to hold the jaw—not the screws. Jaws should be located about 13 to 16 inches from forward end of boom.

The best material for halyards for hoisting the sail to

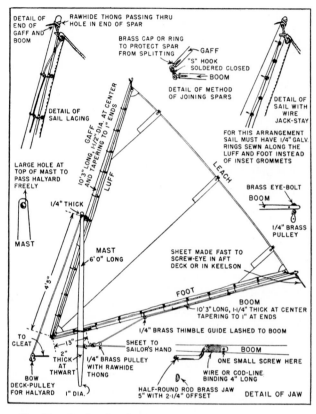

22. Details of sail and rigging.

the mast, is smooth white sash-cord. Fasten this to the gaff about 4 feet above the lower end, using a clove-hitch with an extra turn—no screws.

The mast should be spruce 6 feet high and 2 inches thick where it passes through the supporting thwart;

taper to 1 inch at the top and bottom. Bore the top
with a plain large hole to take the halyard easily. No
block or pulley is advisable at this point; the gaff must
be set snug to mast. A rawhide collar may be placed
on the mast to take the wear in the thwart and also
where the jaw of the boom chafes it. Such a collar
must be fastened without nails—nails break the fibers
of the wood and if long, they meet in a point and cut
the strength of the wood like perforations in a piece of
paper. Sew the collar to a snug fit and then force it
on while wet; it will shrink on tight and may be
further secured by whipping.

The halyard should be adjusted on the gaff so that
the forward ends of the spars just comfortably clear
the gunwales of the canoe, and the boom has just
sufficient rake to clear your head comfortably when
lying against the aft thwart.

For the sheet, a length of soft laid cotton line, ¼ inch
is the best. This will not stiffen when wet and will run
free even in light winds. Secure one end of it to an eye
in the keel well astern; use a brass snap-hook if you
wish. Then lead it up to two or three lignumvitae
dead-eyes fastened along the under side of the boom;
then through a small brass block to your hand. *Never*
cleat the sheet in a canoe. The brass block is best
fastened to a grommet just large enough to slip nicely
on the mast above the thwart, or it may be permanently fastened to the thwart that holds the mast.
Locate one of the dead-eyes on the boom directly over
the leeboard, and the other directly over your head

so that the sheet is held free of everything when coming-about or gybing. This arrangement of the sheet is much more practical and safer than the usual style of leading it directly from the end of the boom to your hand.

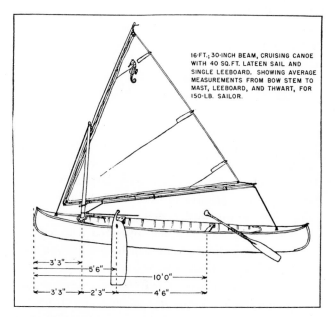

16-FT.; 30-INCH BEAM, CRUISING CANOE WITH 40 SQ. FT. LATEEN SAIL AND SINGLE LEEBOARD. SHOWING AVERAGE MEASUREMENTS FROM BOW STEM TO MAST, LEEBOARD, AND THWART, FOR 150-LB. SAILOR.

23.   Canoe with sail and leeboard.

Leeboards are made of Spanish cedar, mahogany or, if necessary, of spruce. Mahogany is best worked. Material should be 1 inch thick. Boards are 36 inches long from end to hole, and 9 inches wide at the widest point. Fairly straight on the leading edge, also fairly thick and rounded on this edge. The trailing edge may be as thin as desired. The upper end or handle may be finished as desired. This style is most convenient, as it permits operating the boards with your feet when coming about. Only the leeward board is down when sailing. If running free, both boards are up. These boards project about 21 inches below the bottom of the average canoe. The leading edge of the board is thick and round to stand accidental contact with driftwood and to avoid vibration at high speed in a stiff blow. The board tapers to the bottom and to rear edge.

The cross-bar is of ash or oak with two threaded L-hooks to engage underneath the gunwales inside the canoe and hold the bar in place by friction. The bar is stoutly made with two heavy lag screws, brass, set in the bearing faces to carry the leeboards. These lag screws are threaded with a machine thread on the exposed end of the shank and provided with a heavy brass washer and wing-nut which can be tightened sufficiently to hold the leeboard either up or down in any desired position, yet it is free to swing up in case of running into driftwood or shallow water. It usually is necessary to use a wing-nut and a lock-nut, in order to keep the adjustment from working loose after several hours of sailing in a race.

SAILING THE CANOE

So much for the rig! Next, fitting it to the canoe and figuring out the balance. The most practical method (outside of the lengthy and intricate figuring of a designer) is to locate the mast at a convenient thwart as nearly as possible 3 feet 3 inches from the forward stem for a 17-foot canoe. Then figure on sailing in a reclining position, or a sitting position on the bottom, as you prefer, using a thwart located as nearly as possible about one-third the length of the canoe from the stern. Now place the leeboards temporarily about 2 feet 3 inches abaft the mast. Pick a day when there is a smart, steady breeze without much of a sea and set her on a course pointing fairly well into the wind; having your leeboard *straight* down, and sit in the position in which you intend to sail regularly. Take your steering paddle out of the water and see how nearly she will hold her course. If she rounds up into the wind, move the leeboards slightly further aft. If she falls off before the wind, move the boards forward. Experiment with her in this way until you get the boards located exactly at the balancing point, so that she will hold her course fairly steadily, and so that when you shift your own weight slightly forward, she will round into the wind, and by leaning back over the thwart, she will fall off.

Having located the exact balancing point, move the boards permanently just a trifle forward, so that she will have just a comfortable tendency to round into the wind with the boards straight down. You will then be able to sail her with little or no strain on the steering paddle, and will therefore be getting the utmost in her speed; by slanting the leeboards slightly forward or backward, you can vary the balance just a bit as you desire for long beats to windward.

Keep your sail trimmed, so that there is a slight tremble or flutter in the luff—along the gaff. Sail her as nearly as possible flat on her model without heeling over; canoes travel fastest in this way. Hold her down by lying on the gunwale if necessary, and swing one leg out over the water; don't attempt to sit on the gunwale to hold her down. Wind resistance against your body retards your speed in the first place, and second, you'll be spilled out some day by running into sudden dead pocket in the wind.

Steer with a good stiff spruce paddle; serve the shaft, if necessary, to keep it from slipping along the gunwale.

9

Canoeing for the Sportsman and Woodsman

Though the hunter or fisherman might glean all the information he needs from other parts of this book by careful reading, he rates the honor of a separate chapter. Conversely this chapter might be ignored by other specialists, though anyone who takes canoe trips can profit by studying sportsmen's canoeing.

The sportsman paddles his canoe, poles it, tows it, and observes safety precautions just like any other canoeist on a trip. But he selects his model with his special needs in mind. Whatever the virtues of small, light canoes for other purposes, he will usually demand a rugged craft. If long-distance portaging demands a very light boat, that is a situation to be dealt with as met.

THE HUNTER'S CANOE

My Canadian experience showed that, over thousands of square miles, no hunting boats whatever except canoes were in use. Further, the hunters were as skilled as exist anywhere.

I firmly insist that all sportsmen's needs for a hand-propelled or light-motor-propelled boat may be met by some type of canoe. It takes the exception to prove the rule, and those of us who are trained in the natural sciences must admit that exceptions exist, whether or not they are mentioned. The exception here might be the sink box of the waterfowl hunter in coastal marshes.

In many places sink boxes are of questionable legality, or just unquestionably illegal. They are well known to waterfowl hunters and of no interest to others, so a description is unnecessary. They are used as blinds where there is no emergent vegetation or other means for camouflaging a boat that rises appreciably above the water.

Where there is any cover at all, a canoe is just as good as any other boat from the standpoint of conceal-ment, and better in all other respects so far as my experience can show. I spent five years in the Missis-sippi bottoms of Minnesota and Wisconsin, and have made close observations in Canada. I carefully com-pared canoes with all manner of other duck boats.

For the ordinary hunter a medium-sized, sturdy canoe is suggested. My old Prospector Model, made by the Canadian Canoe Company of Peterborough, Ontario, could not be improved on for a party of two. It is 16 feet long, has a 36-inch beam, is 14 inches deep, and leaves 4 inches of freeboard with a load of 850 pounds. It weighs 85 pounds clean and dry—five pounds more with an attached yoke and one paddle.

Another very satisfactory canoe that I used on the Upper Mississippi Wildlife Refuge was a slightly shallower but longer craft, made by the E. M. White Canoe Company of Old Town, Maine. It was a Guide's Special, 18½ feet long but about the same weight as the Prospector.

Both of these canoes were made of canvas-covered cedar, painted about the color of dead marsh vegetation. Mammals—excepting man—may all be color blind, but waterfowl are not handicapped by any impairments of vision so far as I can find out. Some duck hunters do careful camouflage paint jobs on their canoes. This is a matter of individual preference which needs no comment here, except to note that the paint should not shine.

If an aluminum canoe is used, it should be painted or partly painted. A somewhat weathered aluminum boat with dull green markings of standard camouflage type is very inconspicuous.

You rarely worry about the noise of an aluminum boat while duck hunting, but if you are sneaking up a creek for a shot at a smart buck, the canvas-covered canoe has certain advantages. Big-game canoe hunting is the only sporting activity I can envision in which I feel the aluminum boat is at a disadvantage.

Under certain circumstances, with two or more

hunters working together, a twenty-foot Guide's Model is not out of place. In general, however, only one hunter should shoot from a canoe or any other small boat while it is in motion. If the canoe is hidden in the tules, two hunters may shoot sitting back to back. I have occasionally transported four hunters to a waterfowl shooting spot, but they all shot from the shore, and the canoe was used only to put out decoys and gather birds as they fell.

Perhaps we should make some comparison of the canoe and the so-called "duck boat." There are places where duck boats are very popular. I certainly do not want to injure duck-boat sales, but I have never seen anything done with a duck boat that I could not do more easily with a canoe. Further, the canoe is more versatile for other purposes. My old Canadian has been used for fishing and cruising from its native Ontario through Michigan, Wisconsin, Minnesota, Montana, Nevada, California, Oregon, Idaho and Wyoming. It has also been used to shoot ducks, geese, pheasants, deer, and various "varmints."

The pheasant shooting, if you are curious, was largely restricted to the Milk River in Montana, while I was stationed on the Fort Peck Game Range. The Milk is a meandering little stream, flanked by almost impenetrable brush. Smart cock pheasants would hop from one bank to the other, quite safe from brush-foundered hunters. But when we hunted as a party of four, one on each bank and two in the canoe, those cocks were hopping right in front of the bow gunner.

He got most of the shooting, of course, so we had to take turns. Most of the birds fell in the water, where they were easily retrieved.

Even on pretty big water, the canoe has real advantages as a hunting craft. My experience on the Mississippi above Winona, Minnesota, where I was biologist for the Upper Mississippi Refuge, shows this. At that point the river comes down through three great "Pools"—the Winona, the Whitman, and the Alma—that are formed by the dams of the Nine Foot Channel, built in the 1930's. Ducks congregate on these waters, sometimes on one, sometimes another, sometimes all three. You never know where they are until you look. Since there's no law restricting them to one place, it's frequently a case of "here today and gone tomorrow."

This made an almost impossible situation for one of my associates, whom I will call Mr. Smith. He liked duck hunting, and he had a boat all right. It was a good solid craft to shoot from too, being modeled more or less on the lines of a baby flat-top. It was a great pine-planked barge, only slightly smaller than Noah's Ark, and so cumbersome that it took four strong men and a boy to hoist it up on a truck or unload it into the water. Once it reached an anchorage, that was it for the season. Shifting it was an advanced maritime operation much too complicated to repeat twice in one year. You couldn't move it overland from channel to channel. You couldn't pole it through a sticky marsh. You couldn't even row it faster than a mile an hour unless you were really racing. Smith ran it with a big outboard motor, and that limited his operations to the deeper sloughs. He made the mistake of putting this barge down in the Winona Pool one year when the ducks chose to avoid that particular water; and there he had to hunt right through the season, though usually there wasn't a quacker within a country mile.

Meanwhile I, in the canoe, got around in these pools at my pleasure. I could cross all three of them in one day quite easily. I could snatch my 85-pound Guide's Model from channel to channel, pole her or drag her across shallows, or muddy marshes, and paddle her across open water. Of equal importance, I could start all even with Mr. Smith at the close of the shooting day, and pole or paddle my canoe to the parking place much quicker than he could attach his egg beater and come in under power.

I leave it to you to guess who had the best shooting that year.

At this point I should note that it is not legal to shoot from a boat propelled by any means except manual power. This has long been a Federal law as regards migratory-bird shooting, and I believe that all the States and all the Canadian Provinces have similar statutes. In most instances, law-enforcement officers consider that any boat or canoe with a motor attached is "motor-propelled"; so you cannot shoot from an outboard-equipped craft unless you detach the motor from the stern and bring it inboard. At one time the

Minnesota authorities would not even permit shooting from a boat if an outboard engine was lying flat in its bottom; but this law was changed, and I never heard of any other so strict.

It is easy to mount an outboard motor on any canoe big enough for hunting, as I have explained elsewhere in this book. But it is rare for the canoe hunter to really need a motor. Put-putting the canoe is just transportation. The egg beater is most valuable if you use it only to go to the shooting area before shooting hours, and to return after the day ends. A good canoe hunter should get his limit of ducks without using that much time!

In Idaho, since 1948, some of our deadliest duck shooting has been done from a moving canoe. The bow gunner is eligible to shoot as soon as anything is within range. When or if he paddles, he should tie a strong string some four feet long around the middle of the paddle, and fasten the other end through the gunwale on the paddling side. Then he can safely drop the paddle and grab the gun if a duck jumps. It is obviously much faster if the bow gunner is not paddling and is already holding the gun. I have occasionally jump-shot alone in a canoe, by dropping the paddle and grabbing a gun.

An old Canadian hunters' trick is to put a screen of balsam boughs in the bow of the canoe and drift down wind or down current on game. And of course a good paddler can steer the canoe and make some dead-water progress without taking the paddle out of the water, or making other than most limited hand motions. This is something that anyone can learn.

The hunter's canoe should always be equipped with a built-in carrying yoke. Besides paddles, the equipment should include an ordinary setting pole and a duck-bill pole. A good bow ring with a canoe-length ⅜-inch rope attached is desirable on any canoe, but essential for hunting.

THE FISHERMAN'S CANOE

Nearly any canoe suitable for hunting is just as suitable for fishing, but some fishermen insist on an outboard motor while the hunter rarely needs one. Many anglers would do better if they paddled more and motored less.

Canoes are frequently used to work out from big motorboats. My old Canadian has been in on the death of many a bass on the Nevada side of Lake Mead. We lugged it across as a deck load, and then bait-cast on the less-fished areas well away from the landing near Boulder City. We have done the same on Lake Superior and Hudson's Bay. On the latter body of water, two freight canoes were carried lashed to the stays of a 45-foot auxiliary schooner. They were used as lighters and tenders, as well as hunting and fishing boats.

A word may be in order here concerning folding canoes, and the rubber rafts or boats that have been so popular as war surplus. Folding canoes, or collapsible boats of any sort, can be lugged into a remote

region on a pack animal. Experienced packers have put
everything from kitchen stoves to grand pianos on pack
mules, but I have yet to see an animal pack a canoe.
It might be done, but I started horse packing thirty
years too late to try it. Though folding and pneumatic

24. Salmon fishing in New Brunswick from a 22-foot canoe
called a Gaspé.

boats have their places, I do not want to use them any
more than I have to. But anything that will float may
come in handy for fishing, and the poorest canoe substitute is better than nothing.

Years ago in eastern Canada it was a common
practice to make a dug-out canoe—also called a log-
canoe or a pirogue—on a remote lake, and leave it
there when the fishing trip was over. I have seen fine
pirogues made from aspen, white pine, arbor vitae, and

western red cedar. In the South I know they have been made from bald cypress and red gum, and tropical natives make them from many types of hardwood. An axe, an auger, and an adz are the only tools required to make a pirogue. I have seen good ones made with no tools whatever except an axe and a crooked knife. Aboriginals made them by burning and scraping. As to making one myself—all I have done is talk!

As to the choice of a fisherman's canoe, for a lone wolf or a pair of anglers, my Prospector has done just as well for fishing as for hunting. All the suggestions for hunting apply equally to fishing. Inland fish can be caught more easily and played more safely from a canoe than from any other floating device. Canoes are not for deep-sea trolling, or for fishing the largest lakes, unless they work out from a bigger vessel. But in general fishing, no hardship would be experienced if no small boats other than canoes existed.

OTHER PRACTICAL SPECIALTIES

Prospectors, surveyors, game wardens, fire patrolmen, field biologists, trappers, and what-have-you all find the canoe to be the most useful small boat under most conditions.

Army assault boats are essentially canoes, and my heart bleeds to see the way most soldiers paddle them. The use of canoes in mobile warfare in wet countries has been badly neglected, and they have been equally neglected in certain types of rescue work. Our Armed

Services may not own a real canoe, yet a long chapter if not a small book could well be devoted to the military possibilities of canoes. Like pigeons and dogs, they would always be useful, but thus far no one in authority has given them much thought.

10

Canoeing Standards for Camps and Organized Groups

From the beginning of organized camping in this country, those in charge have been deeply concerned for the safety of the people—mostly young, and mostly green in the ways of the woods and waters—who have been entrusted to their care. They have been equally concerned with the courses and methods of instruction in the outdoor arts that form the basis of most camp activity—woodcraft, swimming, canoeing and the like. As a result, all the major camping organizations have developed definite standards of their own, and committed them to print.

The canoeing standards of the four principal groups —the American Camping Association, the Boy Scouts, the Girl Scouts, and the Camp Fire Girls—are printed *verbatim* in the Appendix of this book, for the encouragement and assistance of camps, schools and clubs which wish to give canoeing a suitable activity status.

I have been more or less intimately concerned with organized canoeing off and on since 1915, when I first began to study standards such as these. And, as the

reader of this volume is aware by now, there are ways
in which I do not find any of the present published
standards to be entirely satisfactory. They place, I
think, a disproportionate emphasis on skill in swimming as an aspect of a canoeing program. And they
add needless complexity to some facets of canoe management, while not going far enough in others. My
own suggested canoeing standards, which are ap-
pended at the end of this chapter, try to reduce matters to a better balance. It will be seen that, in many
(but not all) particulars, they closely parallel the
standards of the American Camping Association. As a
matter of fact, I helped work out those standards in
their original version.

THE FACTOR OF SAFETY

Man is a terrestrial animal. Under certain conditions
he may be somewhat arboreal in his habits. Given the
opportunity, he is definitely aquatic to some degree.
Virtually every people with access to water has developed the use of boats. Many tropical natives have been
good swimmers since time immemorial, though the
white races have been slow to develop universal swimming, and it has become established in this country
only during my lifetime. There are still northern races,
such as the Canadian aboriginals, who are perhaps the
world's finest canoeists but who cannot swim at all.
Where they live, water conditions are such that no one
could swim long enough to do much good.

Now everyone knows that water, although a vital

and wonderful servant to humanity in some ways, is lethally dangerous in others. If you are dropped into the depths with nothing to float you, and with no knowledge of swimming, you will drown. It's as simple as that.

It is also true that an improperly trained or reckless paddler—or passenger!—can upset a canoe and spill its occupants into the water. In the past century many white men's canoes were made for specialists and were used by ill-trained people, and there were too-frequent drownings. From this situation, there arose a widespread and unreasoned fear of canoeing.

As a boy, I knew many people who were terrified by canoes, and considered them nothing but instruments of death. These were not all stupid people by any means. My father was one of these extremists, and I am sure that his intelligence was average or better. His understanding of the subject was *nil,* but his opinions were vociferous! As professional canoeing knowledge sneaked up on me, he could never comprehend why I did not drown, or even upset. To the day of his death, he was never in a canoe.

The first canoeing standards arose against a background like that, and I have seen some of them in which the so-called "canoe tests" were swimming tests and nothing else. I must emphasize that I have never known a canoeist who had any objection to camp swimming and life-saving programs, which are in themselves excellent and essential to their purposes. Everyone should learn to swim, just as everyone should learn to read, and at about the same age. But I repeat what I attempted to show in Chapter 3—that swimming skill alone is not a guarantee of absolute safety for the canoeist.

Canoeing skill and experienced canoeing judgment are even more necessary. As I have said before, the Crees and Eskimos paddle all their lives in Arctic waters, often miles from land on wide-open bays, without an upset. I have known Canadian canoemen who paddled probably a thousand miles a year for forty years and never got into trouble. My own experience has not been quite that great, but I have never needed to swim. No canoeist should ever need to swim. What is needed is not less emphasis on swimming—how to save yourself after upsetting—but greater emphasis on the acquisition of canoeing skill and judgment—how to keep yourself from upsetting in the first place.

CANOE MANAGEMENT

In this matter, there are several more or less unrelated ways in which existing canoeing standards should be improved.

First and simplest, the strokes as they are listed are not clearly named. This subject has been discussed in Chapter 4, and needs no enlargement here.

Equally simple is the matter of the strokes that are designated to be taught to learners. This too was discussed earlier; but at the risk of being tedious I shall repeat that the standard lists are confusing in the number of strokes they cover, and that most of these are unnecessary. One list before me includes ten bow strokes and four stern strokes. These admittedly exist, and you could conjure up twice as many if you wished. You would thus create twice as much needless confusion. Four basic strokes, and the means of joining them in purposeful combinations, are all that are really essential.

I note, too, certain omissions in some of the standards as published. One of them, for example, lists portaging as a subject for "discussion." But it does not hold the canoeing instructor—even the head instructor—to any proven minimum of portaging ability. Admittedly special consideration must be given to women packers, but any man who cannot pick up a canoe alone, and lug it half a mile in ten minutes, is not much of a canoeist.

There are sins of commission, too, in such matters as the strict qualifications in swimming skills set up for canoeing instructors. These skills are highly desirable of course, but are they necessary? Would an otherwise expert canoeing teacher be barred from a camp assignment solely because he had never passed any swimming examination? Where an expert camp director is concerned, the answer is "No." For twelve seasons I was head canoeing counselor in the finest of the privately-owned camps, and a consultant for ten seasons more, and I have never taken a swimming examination. I have been associated with two guides who were first-rate instructors, and far better canoeists than I am. They too were with top-flight camps, and so far as I know they never went into the water unless they fell in. I believe that the standard qualifications were quite properly ignored in those cases, but the matter brings up a basic question. If the stated requirements are going to be waived at times, should they be listed at all?

SWIMMING—OR CANOEING?

This leads to a general question about camp canoeing standards as published. Should they be set up, as they apparently are, as an adjunct to the swimming program? In many camps that I have studied, nothing has been planned and managed as well as the swimming and life-saving programs. Nothing has been done as poorly as the canoeing. The swimming is good because it has been worked out by expert swimmers. The canoeing is often bad for exactly the same reason!

A careful study of the records will show that canoeing is now standing on its own feet better than it did twenty, thirty, or forty years ago. But more progress is possible and logical.

I did a little coaching in 1916 and 1917. At that time —and at some camps where I worked as late as 1925— the rules said that no one would be permitted to enter a canoe, even for paddling instruction, until he had passed so-called "canoe tests." These were not in fact canoe tests at all, but swimming tests. The regulations were so strictly enforced that non-swimming campers could not enter even 35-foot war canoes. It would be hard to find anything more stable than these broad-beamed craft; but they bore the dreaded name "canoe" and were therefore "dangerous." On the other hand there were no rules governing the use of some small rowboats we had—fourteen-footers, double-ended, canvas-covered, and built like small canoes with oar-locks. But they were "boats," and therefore they were "safe." The way around this situation, incidentally, was easy. I put non-swimming neophytes in these canvas-covered rowboats and taught them to paddle. Every-one was happy, if foolish. It would have been better, and safer, to use the war canoes. A paddling barge would have been better yet.

Nowadays canoeing regulations are often inter-preted, as they should be, in such a manner that non-swimmers may learn to paddle under careful supervision. All the camps I worked for, after certain head-shakings, tongue-cluckings, and other delaying actions, got around to letting me teach non-swimmers with existing equipment. Sometimes this equipment included ordinary canoes, and narrower, more tippy canoes than I would have chosen. But the good in-structor can—and must—always keep his teaching within safe limits.

Before leaving this discussion of standards, I must again emphasize that no one should upset a canoe, ever, except as a stunt. A horseman cannot ride with-out an occasional fall. ("There was never a hoss that couldn't be rode, There was never a rider that couldn't be throwed!") There are few old airplane pilots who haven't saved their skins by bailing out or by belly-landing. I have yet to meet a really experienced hunter who hasn't had a gun go off accidentally. There is hardly a motorist who hasn't at least brushed fenders or locked bumpers with another car, though the fault may not have been his own. But nothing like this will happen to the canoeist unless he lets it. It has never happened to the many Canadian, Indian, and Eskimo canoemen I have known, and it has never happened to me.

And I repeat for the millionth time that I am all for swimming, as long as you do not *depend* on swimming —not even three strokes—as a safety measure in canoeing.

CANOEING STANDARDS

Permissions at Camps or Schools

Responsible people should be designated to give canoeing permissions, limit the boundaries for paddling, and state the length of time canoes are to be out.

Paddlers should be classified and listed, so that a waterfront director can determine by looking at a chart the exact status of any camper who asks to use a canoe.

One person should accept responsibility for each canoe that goes out.

Care should be taken that unqualified paddlers are kept out of canoes except for purposes of instruction. This applies *especially* to inexpert parents, visitors, and camp help.

When canoes are brought ashore, those who are responsible should at once check in with the person who gave them permission to go out.

A definite signal should be arranged that summons all canoes ashore *at once* when the waterfront director makes such a signal.

The Classification of Paddlers

The following classification is suggested for canoeists:

Class D. Beginners. May go into canoes solely for instruction.

Class C. Elementary canoeists. May not enter a canoe, unless accompanied by a responsible counselor.

Class B. Intermediate canoeists. May use canoes with members of their own or a higher class, under supervision of a canoeing counselor.

Class A. Advanced canoeists. May use canoes alone, or under any arrangement made with the Head Canoeing Counselor. (Similar tests may qualify persons of sufficient maturity as Assistant Canoeing Counselors.)

Class AA. Head Canoeing Counselor.

Class AAA. Canoeing Examiner. May be somewhat honorary in character, and is the highest rating possible.

All canoeists should be classified by these standards, subject to promotion or demotion. Tests may be taken each year. No rating should be considered permanent unless it has been earned at least three times during a period of three years or more. Head Canoeing Counselors should be certified only by Canoeing Examiners, or by a canoeing staff that includes at least one Canoeing Examiner.

Class D. Beginners

Class D paddlers are the crudest beginners. They are to be taught bow paddling or forward paddling only, as outlined in Chapter 4, and preferably from a barge or war canoe. They may be nonswimmers, their canoeing instruction and swimming instruction proceeding simultaneously. They may not enter a canoe unless it is at least 18 feet long, 36 inches wide, and 13 inches deep amidships. Not more than one nonswimmer at a time shall be allowed in any canoe, unless it is a war canoe.

Class D paddlers may enter a canoe only with a properly qualified canoeing counselor, on water that is known to be absolutely safe. This usually means shallow water where there is no wind.

Class C. Elementary Canoeists

Paddlers in all classes from C higher must show by certificate that they are organically sound, and capable of learning strenuous canoeing.

Safety Training. Be able to keep up for fifteen minutes—in a bathing suit—swimming, floating, and treading water by turns.*

* This is a routine safety measure, and should be handled by the swimming staff.

Fall out of a canoe, wearing camp clothes, and hang on until rescued—a minimum of ten minutes.

Be familiar with the fact that canoes float, and that, after an accident, one should cling to the boat, or lie inside it with the face out and the gunwales awash.

Equipment. Be able to care for equipment to the extent of launching and landing properly, knowing how to get in and out of the canoe, turning the canoe over in the shade when necessary, keeping the canoe clean, and taking care of the paddles while doing these things.

Understand construction to the extent of being able to name all parts and materials of which the canoe and paddles are made, and be able to determine whether or not the equipment is safe and of the proper materials and size for the camper in question.

Know that a beginning paddler should kneel, the reason for kneeling, and the right type of kneeling cushion or pad.

Paddling Technique. Learn the four elementary strokes listed in Chapter 4. Paddle them satisfactorily in the bow of a tandem crew, or bow, two or three in a "four," or any position except stern in a war canoe. Too much may not be expected of a Class C paddler in the bow of a war canoe.

Endurance (in tandem or four). Paddle continuously at least two miles, changing sides when requested, covering the distance in forty minutes or less. Smooth water is assumed.

Paddle a total of at least ten miles in a day.

Advanced Safety Training. Test carrying capacity of canoes, with live load, and determine how many people can be supported with the gunwales awash.

Discuss the importance of an extra paddle.

Study methods of changing places in a canoe. (Emphasized in many camps; but there are few, if any, records of an actual necessity for such changing of places, and it should rarely be done in deep water.)

Be tipped out unexpectedly from bow, with counselor in stern. Retrieve paddle, remove clothes, put everything into the canoe, and swim *with the canoe* at least fifty yards to shore.

Class Discussion. Covers important canoeing vocabulary, safety factors, weather conditions, and any other points the instructor deems essential in canoeing fundamentals.

Class B. Intermediate Canoeists

Prerequisite Knowledge. The content of Class C.

Safety Training. Know how to "shake out" and "splash out" a canoe with gunwales awash. Hand-paddle it to shore after emptying it.

Proceed with swimming and life-saving as rapidly as possible. Junior Red Cross Life Saving or its equivalent is highly desirable in this class, but not absolutely necessary.

Practice simple stunts, such as jouncing and gunwale paddling, for developing sense of balance and acquaintance with the canoe.

Study weather, and the canoe's carrying capacity in difficult weather.

Paddling. Master the stern steering stroke ("J" stroke) (No. 5, Chap. 4). Be able to command a crew of four as well as a tandem crew, getting the canoe out smoothly, paddling where the instructor indicates, and bringing the canoe back and properly taking care of it.

Paddle a "figure eight" from each side of the canoe.

Tandem-paddle around a float not larger than ten by fifteen feet, keeping within three feet of the corners, the bow not steering, and land on the "fifth" side, in a way that is satisfactory to the instructor. Repeat, paddling in the opposite direction.

Make satisfactory landing on dock, beach, and rocky shore, under the direction of an instructor.

Paddle a straight course of half a mile, bowman not steering, in a steady rhythm. In bad weather, a deviation of 25 yards is permissible. In calm weather, there should not be more than ten yards' deviation.

Master whatever instructions are given relative to theory of wind, waves, and current.

Get definite practice in a winding stream, with difficult obstructions, if this is possible. Emphasize bow steering in this connection.

Paddle *single,* but with a passenger for ballast, a reasonably straight course, one-fourth mile and return, without changing sides. Repeat, paddling on the other side of the canoe.

Endurance. Paddle in tandem at least twenty miles in one day.

Paddle in tandem five miles, changing sides when requested, in one hour and forty minutes or less.

Portaging Canoe. Learn the procedure, and how a crew of four can carry a canoe in their hands. (Boys under sixteen will not be *expected* to carry canoes alone. Girls will not be expected to carry them alone at all.)

Class Discussion. Covers canoeing literature, and all the points indicated by this Class B outline. Stresses safety training at all times.

Class A. Advanced Canoeists or Assistant Canoeing Counselors

This class is the highest for campers, yet lowest for canoeing counselors. Tests for campers will be exactly the same as for counselors with the exception that the teaching tests will be omitted. Counselors will be expected to have an elementary knowledge of canoe trip essentials. They will also have to demonstrate proper nervous and temperamental control, as well as correct canoeing technique.

Prerequisite Knowledge. The contents of Classes C and B, and Senior Red Cross Life Saving, or its equivalent.

Paddling. Demonstrate *and analyze* all strokes listed in Chapter 4. Demonstration includes sitting, kneeling, and standing positions.

Clearly understand the dynamics of power as exhibited by the paddle forward and aft of the center.

Be an efficient single paddler, without ballast, under varying conditions as suggested by the instructor.

Duplicate the dock landing test under Class B, paddling alone and without ballast. Repeat, paddling bow, with a passenger who does not paddle sitting in the stern and acting as ballast.

Paddle single a triangular course, one-fourth mile on each leg, both with and without ballast, paddling starboard. Repeat the test, paddling port. (The course must be sufficiently straight and the precision must be such that the instructor is satisfied.)

Run at least a mile of fairly difficult rapids. Ascend a sufficient length of rapids to satisfy the instructor that the technique is known. (This assumes poling as well as paddling.)

Endurance.   Paddle alone for an hour, covering at least three miles.

Portaging.   Methods of transportation as well as carrying. Men who are canoeing counselor candidates shall carry a canoe weighing not less than 65 pounds a distance of half a mile in not more than fifteen minutes. The candidate is to pick up the canoe alone, in acceptable form.*

Poling. Understand poling equipment, and the elements of techniques.

---

* I am not prepared to suggest portaging tests for women counselors. Strong women can carry canoes alone; sometimes carry them like handbags, two or four working together.

Sailing. Learn elements, at least in theory.

Class Discussion. Covers all details that are considered in this class; the purchase of canoes and equipment; canoe repair; trip planning and equipment; towing; war canoes; water day programs; canoeing vocabulary and literature.

Trips. Spend at least ten nights on canoe trips for demonstration of the practical points brought up in this class.

Teaching. Teach a minimum of six campers the fundamental strokes and the stern steering stroke listed in Chapter 4.

Teach the essentials of launching and landing, paddle and canoe care, and the elements of crew work, using war canoes too if available.

Teach the elements of safety.

Class AA. Head Canoeing Counselors

Class AA indicates professional canoeing knowledge. Except in rare instances, a minimum of three full seasons of camp training, with an intensive Conference or college course, is necessary before one can assume the responsibility this grade implies. The ability to teach and supervise large groups of canoeists is most important, and an expert canoeing technician may fail if he lacks this essential.

A canoeing expert must know enough general campcraft to plan and organize trips, and he must be able to carry on carefully coordinated activities with the campcraft and nature-study departments. He must also coordinate his work with the swimming department, the latter giving all tests in the water. He should be thoroughly conversant with all material touched upon in this text excepting Chapter 9.

Prerequisite Knowledge. The contents of Classes C, B, and A.

Paddling. Complete the study of double-blade technique and demonstrate mastery of it. (Single-blade technique was completed in Class A.)

Teaching. Teach the remaining strokes, including stunt and controversial strokes not covered in Class A, to a group of at least ten people. Complete any other teaching tests designated by the examiners.

Class Discussion. Covers all points contained in this Class, plus coordination of canoeing with all possible other camp activities.

Also covers first aid and physical care, in collaboration with camp doctor or nurse, for canoeists on trips must be given careful supervision as to their health.

Equipment. Demonstrate complete ability to buy, repair, transport, and in all ways take care of all canoeing equipment.

Organization. Present a satisfactory plan, giving full particulars of all the procedures he would like to develop in his camp, from a list of equipment to details of the longest trips.

Trips. Plan, organize, and direct a six-day trip for twelve people.

Class AAA. Canoeing Examiner

A canoeing examiner may be given that grade only after the unanimous decision of a qualified examining body, the examiners themselves being expert canoeists.

To achieve this class the canoeist must be a recognized authority on canoeing, must have exceptional skill and experience in teaching canoeing, and must have been a Head Canoeing Counselor for at least three years under these or equally rigid requirements.

This is the highest possible canoeing honor, and should be awarded only after the candidate has made an important contribution to canoeing.

A certain flexibility may be possible in standards for the training of canoeing counselors. High standards must be rigidly maintained, but it may be necessary to make exceptions to reach these high standards.

As an example, the life-saving standards may be open to question. The writer, it is repeated, has rated as head canoeing counselor in several excellent camps, in some instances assisted by a canoeing staff of three or more, yet has not taken tests or training in life-saving. This is by no means unusual in woods-trained canoeists, although it is a condition to be avoided if at all practicable, and one which throws extra responsibility on the swimming staff.

No details of the standards will be waived, except after careful consideration, and then only in favor of

individuals known to be well worthy of such exception.

On the other hand, certain people might fulfill to the
letter all the proposed standards, and yet have insufficient ability to do the work that is necessary.

These or other standards are, then, a measure of
possible ability, but should be applied with the discretion that comes only from long experience and careful
study of the subject.

Appendix

THE CANOEING STANDARDS OF
NATIONAL ORGANIZATIONS

The canoeing standards of the four leading national organizations—the American Camping Association, the Boy Scouts, the Girl Scouts, and the Camp Fire Girls—are reproduced in the following pages, with the permission of the respective bodies. Anyone working for one of these groups must of course follow the standards of that group, but familiarity with all of them should prove helpful.

The standards are here reprinted precisely as prepared by the organizations, except that, in the case of the American Camping Association material, the foreword has been omitted and the bibliography combined with the general bibliography of this text. Moreover, the standards of the Camp Fire Girls are those of their general waterfront program, with which their canoeing standards are interwoven.

I call the reader's special attention to the Glossary included in the American Camping Association's material. This is of such excellence that it has saved me the trouble of providing one of my own!

These Standards are of course presented as solely

the work of the several organizations, and they require no individual comment from me. My own views as to what constitute proper and workable canoeing standards for camps and organizations are fully set forth in Chapter 10.

American Camping Association

CANOEING STANDARDS
AND GRADED CLASSIFICATIONS *

Introduction

The underlying purpose of these standards is to stimulate a wider interest in canoeing, by establishing definite standards that aim to point the way to more efficient and safer canoeing by a logical progression in instruction.

Although conditions of water, weather, equipment and program will of necessity vary, the adaptations made to suit the individual situation should not fall below this required minimum.

The primary use of these standards is to serve the canoeing instructor as a guide to a standardized progression of teaching, as well as to act as a means of gauging the progress of the individual student. It also can be used by the director in judging the qualifications of his instructors and the achievements of his canoeing program.

Permissions

PERMISSIONS FOR USING CANOES. A well understood policy should safeguard the use of canoes. A responsible person should always be on duty, at the canoeing area, to give permissions and define boundaries.

* Reprinted with the permission of the American Camping Association.

RATING OF PADDLERS POSTED. The rating and classification of all persons who may use the canoes should be posted where it may be seen by those who give permissions, as well as by those who go out on the water in charge of canoes.

RESPONSIBILITY. The stern paddler should be designated as in charge, whenever a canoe is in use.

IRRESPONSIBLE PADDLERS. There should be a clearly defined policy as to the use of canoes by other than classified paddlers. Inefficient personnel and visitors are a distinct risk and should not be allowed in canoes. Safety interests should outweigh hospitality.

REGISTERING CANOES THAT ARE ON THE WATER. A plan should be devised for registering on a bulletin at the dock the canoes that are out and the individuals who are using them.

CHECKING OFF, immediately upon returning, should be required.

WEATHER SIGNAL. Some sort of sign (as a flag or bulletin) should be used to indicate if the weather is suitable for canoeing and, most important, a signal, as a flag, or loud sound (as a bugle, horn, bell or whistle) should, in any emergency, recall paddlers to shore immediately. All paddlers should know the storm warnings of their area and under unfavorable conditions land immediately on the nearest shore.

TRIP PROCEDURE. On trips, short or long, a similar plan should be used.

Classification of Paddlers

It is desirable to classify paddlers according to skill, knowledge and habitual performance.

Class D

BEGINNING CANOEING

Note: Emphasis in this class is on safety education and basic elementary skills as a foundation for beginners. These paddlers *may go in a canoe only with a qualified canoeing instructor within a restricted area.*

Prerequisites

1. HEALTH. Present a registered MD's certificate stating that the candidate is organically sound.
2. SAFETY TRAINING
   a. *Swimming Test*—Without touching bottom jump or dive into deep water and consecutively, tread water for at least one minute, swim 25 yards and float for at least one minute.
   b. *Tip Test*—Know by demonstrating, with an instructor, that in an upset you NEVER LEAVE YOUR CANOE, but:
      1) climb inside and paddle or handpaddle to shore
      2) cling to it and push it to shore
      3) wait to be rescued

Requirements

The content of the instruction should follow as far as possible the outline of Class C and the aim should be to develop a feeling of security and confidence in and on the water.

Class C

ELEMENTARY CANOEING

Note: Emphasis in this class is on the development of the knowledge of techniques and safety education.

Prerequisites

1. HEALTH. Present a registered MD's certificate stating that the candidate is organically sound.
2. SAFETY TRAINING
   a. *Swimming Test*—A jump into deep water followed by a ten minute swim using either the elementary back, side, or breast stroke.
   b. *Tip Test*—Know by demonstrating each of the following methods with another student that in an upset you NEVER LEAVE YOUR CANOE but:
      1) climb inside and paddle or handpaddle to shore
      2) cling to it and push it to shore
      3) cling to it and wait to be rescued

Requirements

I. EQUIPMENT
   A. *Care of canoe and paddles.* Demonstrate ability to:
      1. take good general care of paddle and canoe
      2. turn canoe over on racks and ground
      3. care for canoe in launching, land and stowing
      4. get in and out of canoe from beach, dock, float and bank
      5. care for paddles and duffle while doing above
   B. *Nomenclature.* Know in enough detail for better understanding in receiving instruction and in actual use the:
      1. parts of a canoe
      2. parts of a paddle
      3. length and weight of paddle for own use
II. TECHNIQUE OF PADDLING
   A. *Strokes.* Demonstrate and explain the following bow strokes
      1. bow stroke
      2. backwater

3. draw
4. push over
5. hold
6. quarter sweep

Note: The above strokes must be passed to qualify a student as a Class C paddler. However it is also assumed that the "J" and backing stroke are also being taught at the same time.

B. *Crew of four.* Paddle as bow, 2 and 3 with a class A paddler or canoeing instructor in the stern. (For training in balance, coordination, rhythm and for economy in teaching.)
C. *Tandem paddling.* Be an efficient bow in fair weather.
D. *Shallow shore.* Explore without running aground and find out how much water the canoe draws.

III. ENDURANCE (TANDEM). Paddle continuously one mile, in good rhythm, changing sides after one-half mile.

IV. SAFETY TRAINING
    A. *Kneeling position.* Know advantages of kneeling (knee cushion should be provided).
    B. *Extra paddle.* Know why an extra paddle should always be taken.
    C. Demonstrate the safe method of changing places bow and passenger (recommend changing places only in shallow water).
    D. Tip over canoe in deep water and push for fifty yards and then demonstrate emptying canoe in shallow water.

V. DISCUSSION ON:
    A. General safety rules
    B. Weather wisdom
    C. Canoeing vocabulary (mutual understanding of commands and terms)

Class B

INTERMEDIATE

Note: Emphasis in this class is on the development of techniques and principles of safe and efficient canoeing.

Prerequisites

1. HEALTH. Present a registered MD's certificate stating that the candidate is organically sound.
   Immediately prior to any overnight trip all participants should have a medical recheck by the physician or nurse.
2. SAFETY TRAINING
   a. *Swimming test*—Jump into deep water, fully clothed (laced shoes or sneakers, long pants, blouse or shirt) disrobe, swim for fifteen minutes using the elementary back stroke, side stroke and breast stroke.
   b. Alone, without either swamping or losing contact with the canoe, jump out in deep water and reenter.
3. CANOEING. Pass requirements for Class C.

Requirements

I. EQUIPMENT
   A. Care. Demonstrate ability to:
      1. land and launch on a rocky shore, beach, float and high bank under varied conditions
      2. care for canoe and paddle while landing and launching on the above
      3. make emergency repairs on canoe and paddle
         a. torn canvas with leak
         b. split paddle blade
         c. broken paddle shaft

B. Construction. Know:
   1. how a canoe is constructed
   2. how to select canoes for different purposes
II. TECHNIQUES
   A. Strokes. Demonstrate and explain all bow and stern strokes (see Appendix).

   Be entirely familiar with each and know under what conditions each is used.

   Note: The above strokes must be passed to qualify a student as a Class B paddler. However it is also assumed that the single paddling stroke and poling will be introduced before a paddler is qualified as Class B.

   B. Crew of four. Cox a crew in:
      1. carrying and launching canoe
      2. getting in and shifting sideward
      3. paddling a straight course in a steady rhythm
      4. holding, backing and making turns
      5. stowing canoe and equipment
   C. Tandem paddling
      1. As bow and stern paddling port and starboard execute:
         a. a figure eight
         b. a course around a float within three feet of the sides
         c. a straight course in steady rhythm under varied weather conditions
      2. Stream and current
         a. As bow and stern paddle up and down a winding stream (or simulated conditions)
         b. Know possible obstructions and how to deal with them.
         c. Understand how to shift weight to meet situations produced by obstructions.
   D. Trips are an important part of a canoeing program

and they should be introduced before a person is
qualified as a Class B paddler.

III. ENDURANCE TANDEM
   A. Paddle continuously five miles changing sides
      every mile.
   B. Paddle a total of ten miles in one day in a
      moderate wind.

IV. SAFETY TRAINING
   A. Emptying a swamped canoe:
      1. at dock
      2. at shore
   B. Demonstrate ability to do a canoe over canoe
      rescue.

V. DISCUSSION
   A. Safety
   B. Underlying principles of steering
   C. Theory of landings
   D. Wind and waves
   E. Streams, currents, rapids
   F. Weather wisdom
   G. Upsets under various circumstances
   H. Canoeing vocabulary
   I. Portaging canoes
   J. Loading canoes (personnel and duffle)

Class A and/or

ASSISTANT CANOEING INSTRUCTOR
Important Notes

1. Emphasis in this class is on more definite skill and
   broader knowledge than in Class B with experience in
   teaching individuals and small groups.
2. Until these Class A standards have been passed each
   candidate's responsibilities and activities should be
   carefully supervised by the head canoeing instructor.

3. A candidate is a person of practical experience on and in the water who has demonstrated satisfactorily sufficient leadership qualities, and control, and care of the canoe under varying conditions.
4. Assistant canoeing instructors should possess essential temperamental qualities, such as responsibility and judgment, a well as mental and physical control.
5. Candidates may be rated as Class A but not as assistant canoeing instructors if they meet all the requirements except those listed under teaching.
6. Campcraft knowledge (namely overnight camping away from base camp) is a prerequisite to canoe trips.

Prerequisites

1. HEALTH. Present a registered MD's certificate stating that the candidate is organically sound.
2. CANOEING KNOWLEDGE. Pass standards for Classes C and B.
3. SAFETY TRAINING.
   a. Assistant canoeing instructors must hold current Royal Life Saving Society, Intercollegiate YMCA, Boy Scout or Red Cross Senior Life Saving certificates, or others of equal difficulty.
   b. Candidates for Class A must hold current certificates for the Junior grade of the above.

Requirements

I. TECHNIQUE OF PADDLING. Analyze, demonstrate (starboard and port) and explain the following:
   A. All strokes (see Appendix). In these demonstrations, explain as well as show, that the effect of the various strokes depends upon:
      1. the angle of the blade in the water
      2. the amount of pressure against the water at any given point
      3. the place at which the stroke starts

      4. the path of the blade in the water

      5. the place where the stroke ends

  B. Tandem paddling

     1. As stern and bow be efficient in wind and rough water for a distance of one mile.

     2. As stern and bow be efficient up and down a winding stream or under simulated conditions.

     3. Demonstrate various styles of paddling (bent upper arm and straight upper arm).

  C. Single paddling

     1. Demonstrate the positions and explain the reasons for paddling in different parts of the canoe.

     2. Demonstrate the mechanical advantages of ballast.

  D. Rapids paddling. (Know in theory if not accessible to rapids.) As bow and stern successfully:

     1. ascend 50 yards of rapids either paddling or poling

     2. run a section of rocky rapids

II. Poling

  A. Equipment

     1. Know choice and construction of pole

       a. wood (ash for flexibility and strength)

       b. length (9-12 feet)

       c. spiked end

       d. one and one-half inches in diameter

     2. Methods of carrying pole in the canoe

  B. Technique

     1. Demonstrate and explain position in canoe when:

       a. alone

       b. with bow man or ballast

       c. going up or downstream or with head and tail wind

    2. Demonstrate and explain grip, propulsion and recovery in shallow water while:
       a. poling
       b. snubbing
       c. turning
    3. In white water or a high wind on a lake demonstrate:
       a. poling and snubbing
       b. loading for traveling with a head or tail wind (or up and downstream)
       c. settings
       d. landings

C. Discussion
    1. Reading white water
    2. Theory of wind, wave, current and weight
    3. Use of bow paddler

III. TEACHING GROUPS (from Classes D, C and B with a minimum of six candidates in each)

A. Strokes. Teach all bow and stern strokes (see Appendix)
    Note: Know that of primary importance is making clear to students why the canoe moves in a certain way with a given stroke.

B. Teaching presentation and progression of:
    1. bow, stern and single paddling
    2. crew of four paddling
    3. war canoe (if equipment is available)

C. Safety Training
    1. Know the value and uses of a rope in a canoe (minimum of 10 feet).
    2. Tandem dumping and climbing in.
    3. Canoe awash
       a. hand paddling
       b. pushing canoe to shore

VI. ENDURANCE

Single paddle continuously one hour, in steady rhythm, in rough water.

V. SAFETY TRAINING

   A. Demonstrate:

      1. how to "shake out" a canoe in deep water
      2. how to "splash out" a canoe in deep water
      3. the buoyancy test to determine how many people it will support clinging to the gunwales or seated in the bottom of a swamped canoe.

   B. Know:

      1. points of a steady canoe
      2. points of an unsteady canoe
      3. that a canoe's carrying capacity depends upon:
         a. age of canoe
         b. ability of paddlers
         c. use in various situations

VI. DISCUSSION

   A. Safety—responsibilities as an instructor
   B. Analysis of strokes, teaching methods and progression
   C. Difference and use of canoes of various models and sizes
   D. Towing—the one safe method
   E. Portaging, alone and with various numbers of assistants; also use of paddles as a yoke, other yokes, canoe wheels and wagon wheels
   F. Trips

      1. Trip planning. Personnel, maps, clothing, equipment and food
      2. Loading canoes with paddlers and duffle
      3. Care of all equipment on trips
      4. Care of health on trips
      5. Campcraft. Minimum campcraft knowledge essential for canoe trips

G. Equipment for Canoeing
   1. Sources, models, prices, selection and ordering
   2. General upkeep and repair
   3. Summer storage—canoe racks, paddle racks
   4. Winter storage
   5. Transportation—portage, automobile, wagon, railroad, steamboat, motorboat
   6. War Canoes—advantages and disadvantages
H. Canoeing literature
I. Canoeing vocabulary

VII. MINIMUM OF TEN NIGHTS ON CANOE TRIPS, satisfactorily demonstrating all above tests.

Class AA

HEAD CANOEING INSTRUCTOR

Important Notes

1. Emphasis in this class is placed on the educational aspects of canoeing; the ability to organize, teach and supervise large groups for a long period of time (as a camp season or college course).
2. A head canoeing instructor should be more experienced on and in the water and have a greater degree of responsibility and judgment.

Prerequisites

1. HEALTH. Present a registered MD's certificate stating that candidate is organically sound.
2. CANOEING KNOWLEDGE. Pass standards for Class C, B and A.
3. SWIMMING. Must hold a current Royal Life Saving Society, Intercollegiate YMCA, Boy Scout or Red Cross Water Safety Instructor certificate or others of equal difficulty.

Requirements

I. TECHNIQUE OF PADDLING
   A. Review all strokes (see Appendix).
   B. Demonstrate double blade paddling explaining advantages and disadvantages.

II. TEACHING
   A. Analyze all strokes (know teaching progression and how to correct common faults).
   B. Teach and demonstrate all material in Classes C, B and A to groups of at least ten.
   C. Explain the reasons for the various safety techniques in Classes C, B and A.

III. PROGRAM. Organization and Administration
   A. Set up a program in any given situation.
   B. Know methods of integrating canoeing program with other activities (swimming, campcraft, nature, hiking, handicraft, art, music, general recreation, etc.)
   C. Plan and present a Water Day Program.
   D. Trips
      1. Organize and conduct several canoeing trips of at least three days each including all having to do with the comfort of the personnel.
      2. Health of campers on trips. Know:
         a. factors that conserve health
         b. nutrition requirements
   E. Canoeing Equipment
      1. Upkeep and repair of canoeing equipment
      2. Make out requisition for materials required with estimate of quantity, probable cost and with regard to use and specific needs.
      3. Plan and lay out a canoeing waterfront.

Class AAA

CANOEING EXAMINER

A canoeing examiner shall be one who has been for three years a Head Canoeing Instructor under these standards, has shown exceptional skill as a teacher, is an authority on types of canoes and equipment and is looked upon as having made a distinct contribution to the field of canoeing.

An examining board will be set up in the New England section and in other sections as the need arises.

APPENDIX

STROKES

The names of the strokes vary in different regions and many of them are variations or combinations of the fundamental strokes. Sometimes two names are used for mere degrees of intensity or speed—as in "circling" and "banking" and it is well to know the various names but convenient to use those that seem to be in more general use. (In the following list the name of the stroke given first is the most common.)

† Since there are many different techniques of paddling it is difficult to reach agreement on exactly how the hands, arms, and body should be used during a stroke. For this reason we have given only the path of the blade through the water in describing the strokes below.

Bow Strokes

1. Bow STROKE (Straight-away). Used to impart forward motion.

   The blade is dipped forward, close to the canoe,

† These are the revised descriptions of strokes as given in the Canoeing Manual, 1952, by the New England Camping Association, Inc., and accepted by the American Camping Association.

and drawn aft until the lower hand is just past the hip, then cut out of the water and feathered forward to the starting point.

2. BACKWATER. Used to impart backward motion.
   This stroke is the reverse of the bow stroke.

3. DRAW STROKE (Pull-to). Used to impart sideward motion toward the paddling side.
   The blade is extended outward directly opposite the hip and parallel to the keel, dipped and drawn toward the hip and just before the paddle touches the canoe the blade is cut aft and feathered back to the starting point. (The stroke may also be done with an underwater recovery.)

†4. PUSH-OVER (Push-away). Used in the bow, stern, or center to impart sideward motion away from the paddling side.
   The paddle is extended to the rear parallel to the gunwale with the edge facing downward, cut into the water to a position opposite the hip, pressed outward until the blade leaves the water, and is then feathered back to the starting position. (An underwater recovery may also be used. To start the stroke the blade is cut into the water from the rear or out from the side to a position close to the canoe, opposite the hip, and perpendicular to the water. The blade is turned and pressed outward, and just before it would leave the water one edge is turned inward, and the blade is cut back to the side of the canoe ready to start the next stroke.)

5. HOLD. To stop.
   Cut the blade into the water to a position perpendicular to the keel and just forward of the hip. Hold!

6. QUARTER SWEEP. To impart sideward motion, with "way" and away from the paddling side.

The blade is dipped forward, close and parallel to the canoe, swept outward describing an arc of 45 degrees and feathered back to starting point.

† For maximum efficiency during all sweep strokes (quarter sweep, half sweep, etc.) the blade during the stroke should always have one edge pointing straight up. If laid at an angle in the water a certain amount of power is lost by the angled blade pressing downward. The wider the sweep of the paddle from the side of the canoe the greater will be the turning effect of the stroke.

7. SCULL. To impart sideward motion, without "way," toward the paddling side.

The paddle is held nearly vertical with the blade extending slightly forward of the hip and the leading edge angled away from the canoe. The blade is drawn aft with the pressure exerted toward the canoe; on the forward stroke the reverse is done so that the leading edge is again angled away from the canoe and pressure is exerted on the same face of the blade.

8. REVERSE SCULL. To impart sideward motion, without "way," away from the paddling side.

† The paddle is held vertical to the side of the canoe with the blade extended slightly forward of the hip. The blade is drawn aft with the leading edge angled slightly inward and pressure exerted away from the canoe; on the forward stroke the reverse is done so that the leading edge is angled inward toward the canoe and pressure is exerted outward. Pressure is therefore exerted on the same face of the blade on the forward and backward part of the stroke.

9. Bow RUDDER. Used to direct motion to the paddling side.

With the paddle held against the gunwale at an angle of 30 to 45 degrees dip and hold.

10. CROSS BOW RUDDER. Used to direct motion away from the paddling side.

The paddle is lifted over the bow of the canoe and placed in the water in a corresponding position to the bow rudder.

Stern Strokes

1. "J." To impart forward motion and guide the direction of the canoe.

The blade is dipped forward, close to the canoe and drawn aft until opposite the hip where the inside edge gradually turns aft and outward with pressure exerted continuously on the same face of the blade. Cut the blade out of the water and feather to starting point.

†2. BACKING (Combination stroke). Used in the center or stern to impart backward motion and guide the direction of the canoe.

The blade is extended backward and slightly away from the side of the canoe (the distance is determined by the amount of correction needed), dipped and pulled to the canoe (draw stroke), turned so that the outer face of the blade is forward, and then pushed forward along the line of the gunwale (backwater stroke). The blade can then be lifted from the water and feathered back to the starting point or turned so that the outer edge is leading and cut through the water back to the starting point.

3. HALF SWEEP. To impart sideward motion, with "way," away from the paddling side.

The blade is extended outward directly opposite the hip and dipped edgewise then pressure is applied aft describing an arc of 90 degrees. The blade is then cut out of the water and feathered back to the starting point.

4. Reverse Half Sweep. To impart sideward motion away from the paddling side with "way" astern.

This stroke is the reverse of the half sweep.

The draw, push-over, scull, reverse scull and hold are also used in the stern.

Single Paddling Strokes

Single paddling strokes are mainly variations or combinations of the following fundamental canoeing strokes:

1. "J"
2. Backwater
3. Draw and push-over
4. Scull and reverse scull

Those peculiar to single paddling are the:

1. Full Sweep (C stroke). To impart turning motion away from the paddling side.

The blade is dipped forward close and parallel to the canoe, swept outward and backward describing an arc of 180 degrees, cut out of the water and feathered forward to the starting point.

2. Reverse Sweep. To impart turning motion toward the paddling side.

This stroke is the reverse of the full sweep.

3. Inverted Sweep. To impart turning motion toward the paddling side.

† The blade is angled with the outer edge diagonally forward and dipped forward and slightly away from the side of the canoe, swept inward and backward scooping in toward the keel and then away from the canoe again, describing an arc of 180 degrees, lifted out of the water, and feathered forward to the starting point. Pressure is exerted on the same face of the blade throughout the stroke.

SAFETY RULES FOR THE INDIVIDUAL

1. Know your own skill and stay within its limits.
2. Never take a non-swimmer out with you.
3. Never "show off." Always play safe, especially in unknown waters.
4. Dress. Wear clothing that could be taken off quickly in an emergency.
5. Do not lean out of a canoe for any reason.
6. Always carry an extra paddle.
7. Always paddle within a half mile of shore.
8. If you upset NEVER LEAVE YOUR CANOE.
9. No canoe should be paddled within a swimming area while there are swimmers in the water.
10. Paddling after dark is not recommended.

STUNTS

Stunts may be included for additional training in balance. They should be done only under controlled conditions and with proper supervision.

GLOSSARY OF TERMS

Aft—Nautical term meaning: toward the stern.

Air Tanks—Chamber built into the sides of the Sponson canoe to give greater stability and into the ends of the aluminum canoe to give buoyancy and seaworthiness.

Bilge—That part of the canoe that is below the waterline.

Bow—The front of the canoe.

Cox—To command the crew.

Cut—To move the paddle in or out of the water with one edge leading.

Deck—A section of wood fitted between the gunwales in the bow and stern for the purpose of bracing and ornamentation.

Displacement—Actual weight of the water displaced by the canoe.

Draft—The vertical distance from the waterline to the keel.

Feather—To recover the paddle over the water with the blade parallel to the surface of the water.

Flare—Point of curvature where the side of the canoe curves to become the bottom.

Floor Boards—False flooring made of slats and used to protect the ribs and planking.

Fore—Nautical term meaning: toward the bow.

Freeboard—The vertical distance of the canoe above the waterline.

Gunwale—Strips of material along the topmost part of each side and extending from bow to stern. Used for bracing and finishing.

Hog—Term used when there is a sag at each end of the canoe.

Hull—The body of the craft.

Inboard—Nautical term meaning inside the line of the craft's hull.

Inwale—Inner part of the gunwale.

Keel—Protecting strip on the outside of the canoe extending along the bottom from stem to stem.

Lee—On the side or in the direction opposite from which the wind is blowing.

Outboard—Nautical term meaning outside the line of the craft's hull.

Outer Stem—Curved piece fitted over the stem on the outside of the canoe.

Outwale—Outer part of the gunwale.

Over-all-length—Measure of distance from stem to stem.

Painter—Rope attached to bow.

Planking—Longitudinal strips of wood fastened over the ribs.

Port—Nautical term meaning left (facing the bow).

Ribs—Curved strips running crosswise from gunwale to gunwale which give the canoe its shape.

Sag—Term used to indicate an excessive drop in the keel line of the canoe.

Starboard—Nautical term meaning right (facing the bow).

Stem—A curved piece of wood fitted into the inside of the bow and stern which gives shape to the ends.

Stem Band—Strip of metal screwed to the outer stem for added protection.

Stern—The rear of the canoe.

Thwart—Piece extending from gunwale to gunwale and used to maintain the shape of the canoe.

Trim—To cause the canoe to assume a balanced position in the water.

Tumblehome—That part of the canoe which curves outward from the vertical line drawn from the gunwale to the bottom of the canoe.

Way—Movement in a forward or backward direction.

Windward—On the side or in the direction from which the wind is blowing.

PARTS OF THE PADDLE

Blade—The flat part of the paddle which provides the propelling surface.

Double Blade—A paddle with blades at both ends of the shaft which may be flat or cupped.

Drip Rings—Rubber rings on the shaft of a double blade paddle to keep the water from dripping on the paddler.

Flare—That section of the paddle where the shaft flattens to become the blade.

Grip—The top end of the shaft which is held by the paddler.

Shaft—Round part of the paddle extending from the grip to the flare.

Tip—The end of the blade.

Throat—That part of the paddle shaft just above the blade.

Boy Scouts of America

CANOEING REQUIREMENTS

To earn the Canoeing Merit Badge you must be a First Class Scout or Explorer, and do the following:

1. With a companion of about your weight, and using a canoe not less than 14 feet in length:

   a. Launch and get in the canoe properly from pier or shore (both if possible), giving directions to your companion.

   b. Using a single blade paddle while kneeling on one or both knees, in the bow position, paddle 100 yards, turn and paddle back, showing proper form in the following strokes:

Bow Stroke	Reverse Sweep
Diagonal Draw	¼ Sweep Stroke
Push Over	

   c. Change paddle to other side and repeat requirement b.

   d. While your canoe is afloat, properly change places with your companion who will now paddle in the bow. On one or both knees, paddle 100 yards and return, showing ability to keep canoe on straight course.

   e. Make a proper landing.

2. While alone in canoe, using a single-blade paddle, paddle over a 100-yard course and return, demonstrating two kneeling positions for one man, and correctly do the following on one side going out, and on the other side coming back:

J-Stroke	Push Over
Draw Stroke	Stopping

3. While fully dressed: °

   a. Capsize a canoe in deep water and about 50 yards from landing place.

   b. Right it and stow paddle and kneeling pad. Get in and paddle with hands or paddle, for 25 yards.

   c. Disrobe, secure clothing to thwarts, go overboard, and, holding on with one hand, swim and tow, or swim and push swamped canoe to shore.

   d. Properly land emptied canoe and put it away, with assistance if necessary.

4. Using double-blade or single-blade paddle, assist a man who has capsized his canoe and is clinging to it. Empty it as explained in the Merit Badge pamphlet, and steady it while man climbs aboard.

5. Discuss contents of a good emergency canoe repair kit, and explain how to use it in repairing a one-inch hole in canvas.

° Wear clothing usually worn in canoeing in your territory according to the season of year.

CANOEING STANDARDS

Girl Scouts of the United States of America ° °

Small-craft activities should be carried out according to a progressive and well-planned program. There should be group discussion and individual understanding of all waterfront regulations and safety devices and aids. There should also be progressive tests. The group should be familiar with the rules of the road for small craft, correct behavior on board a boat, and nautical ways.

All girls should be classified according to their ability to

° ° Standards for the use of canoes and small boats are given in the program for small-craft activities. Reprinted from *Safety-Wise*, 1940 and 1950, by permission of the Girl Scouts of the United States of America.

handle the specific small craft being used. Every girl, with the exception of those classified as passengers, should demonstrate her ability to meet the basic swimming requirements for boating, which consist in demonstrated ability to jump into deep water, recover calmly, tread water, stay afloat, and swim with ease within a small space range.

Small craft should be used only with permission, in a designated area, in daylight hours, and under the supervision of one or more Senior Life Savers.

Small craft should never be used in adverse weather conditions, such as high winds, fog, or a storm.

Rowing. When a nonswimmer is taken as a passenger in a rowboat, she should be accompanied by a Senior Life Saver, and the boat should be handled by an experienced oarsman.

To enter a boat as a learner, a girl should have successfully completed the basic swimming requirements and be accompanied by an experienced oarsman.

Before entering a boat without an experienced oarsman, a girl should have successfully completed the basic swimming requirements, show some rowing ability, and demonstrate either hand-paddling or some form of paddling or propulsion with a single oar. She should also be able to swamp (not tip) a boat and propel it in swamped condition along shore.†

Canoeing. Before entering a canoe as a passenger or learner with an experienced paddler, a girl should have successfully completed the basic swimming requirements; experienced a canoe tip-over in company with a qualified canoeist; and participated in propelling the canoe along

† To ensure that the learner will regard the boat swamp and canoe tip-over as demonstrations of the application of a principle and not as a form of self-rescue that is good only for a specified distance, the small craft being used should be propelled along shore.

the shore line while using it for support either upside down or right side up.

Before using a canoe without an experienced paddler, a girl should have successfully completed the basic swimming requirements and demonstrated her ability to hand-paddle a canoe, to reasonably control and guide it with a paddle, and finally to tip over and propel it along shore in an acceptable manner.†

In a Girl Scout established or day camp, under the guidance of a waterfront staff, a nonswimmer may handle a rowboat or canoe if she is accompanied by a qualified life saver.

† See footnote on preceding page.

Camp Fire Girls
WATERFRONT STANDARDS *

Personnel—Staff Qualifications

E. Additional requirements for waterfront staff

    1. Director

        a. At least 21 years of age.

        b. Current certification as American Red Cross Water Safety Instructor or its recognized and approved equivalent from the Boy Scouts of America, Y.M.C.A., Canadian Red Cross, or Royal Life Saving Society.

        c. Ability to organize and supervise total waterfront program including swimming and use of water craft.

        d. Previous experience teaching or supervising waterfront activities.

    2. Waterfront counselors must hold current American Red Cross Water Safety Instructor or Senior Life

* Reprinted with the permission of Camp Fire Girls, Inc., from *Resident Camp Standards*, 1952.

Saving certificates or their equivalents as specified above. (Basic qualifications for counselors require minimum age of 19.)

3. There should be one counselor who has the same qualifications as the waterfront director to take over in her absence.

Volunteer Staff

A. All standards for waterfront staff must be met.

Site, Facilities, and Equipment

Facilities and Equipment

G. *Swimming areas*

1. Selection of natural swimming areas, design and construction of waterfront facilities should be done in consultation with American Red Cross or other recognized authorities and should meet their recommendations. (See Life Saving and Water Safety, American Red Cross.)

2. All swimming pools must be constructed so that purification, circulation, and filtration meet the standards of state and local laws. In the absence of such laws, the recommendations of the American Red Cross should be followed. Care should be taken to avoid pollution either through drainage or use.

Health

I. PHYSICAL EXAMINATION

A. All campers and staff must have a physical examination by a licensed doctor of medicine within five days of entering camp and a further check must be made by the camp nurse upon arrival at camp.

Other health standards apply indirectly to waterfront activities.

Safety

I. SAFETY IN PROGRAM ACTIVITIES

A. *Waterfront*

   1. Supervision

      a. All swimming pools and waterfront areas must be under the direct supervision of a person holding a current Water Safety Instructor certificate from the American Red Cross, or its recognized and approved equivalent Boy Scouts, YMCA, Canadian Red Cross, or Royal Life Saving Society.

      b. In addition to the waterfront director there must be at least one qualified assistant for every group of ten swimmers (currently certified American Red Cross Water Safety Instructor or Senior Life Saver or equivalent as specified above).

      c. All waterfront activities must be supervised at all times by waterfront staff.

   2. Equipment must conform to American Red Cross recommendations or other recognized standards.

      a. Life Saving equipment must be kept in perfect order at all times and be quickly and easily accessible. It should include: emergency bell, life boat, ring buoys, bamboo poles, surf board, and other helpful equipment.

      b. Slippery surfaces of docks, diving boards, and floats must be covered with nonskid paint, matting, or canvas.

      c. Watercraft must be kept in safe condition and must be properly equipped.

   3. Safety regulations

      a. Swimming areas must be kept clean and free from hidden dangers; known hazards must be safeguarded.

b. Swimming area must be divided into areas for swimmers of varying abilities and clearly marked with flags, ropes, or other devices for safety. Swimmers must stay in their own areas.

c. Overcrowding of the swimming area must be avoided.

d. Check board and buddy systems must be in force in all swimming areas with the addition of boat patrol in natural areas such as lakes or rivers. Swimmers might also be identified as to swimming ability (colored caps).

e. There must be no swimming or boating alone.

f. No watercraft other than life boats must be allowed in swimming area during swimming periods.

g. Watercraft must not be overloaded.

h. Watercraft must be used only by those qualified to do so and under supervision.

i. For the protection of the camp, visitors must not be permitted to use swimming or boating facilities.

4. When waterfront facilities belonging to another organization or group are used, the same standards must be met.

Following are suggested boating honors which girls may earn in the Camp Fire program; they may choose to do any or all of these activities.

Boating

Before attempting any of these boating honors, a girl must be able to swim 50 yards in water beyond her depth.

301. Demonstrate 2 different canoe strokes in good form.

302. Push off, dock, and beach a canoe correctly.

303. Rig a sail and install a rudder on a canoe and sail for 2 miles.
304. Paddle a canoe for 20 miles in any 5 days. (Younger girls may share paddling with another person.)
305. Demonstrate paddling stern in a canoe using at least 2 strokes.
306. Paddle a canoe Indian fashion. (Do not lift paddle from water.)
307. Demonstrate to an adult leader your ability to tip over canoe in deep water, right it, get in and paddle 100 yards.
308. Row a boat for 20 miles in any 5 days.
309. Post in the boathouse 5 safety rules for boating.
310. With an adult leader take an overnight trip, using a canoe or rowboat for transportation.
311. Keep a log of an overnight boat trip.
312. Sail a boat for 15 miles.
313. Demonstrate safety measures regarding a sail boat.
314. Teach someone else to read a navigation chart for any body of water.
315. Send and receive 3 messages using the signal flag code.
316. Send and receive 3 messages using the wigwag or the flash code.
317. Take a 5-mile kayak trip in shallow water.
318. Take part in gunwale race using a canoe.

BIBLIOGRAPHIES

The bibliographies which follow are arranged in three sections: my own, that included in the Boy Scouts' Merit Badge manual *Canoeing,* and that of the American Camping Association. Entries in my bibliography are numbered to correspond to references in the text of this book. In all bibliographies, titles believed or known to be out of print are marked with an asterisk (*); those which appear in more than one of the lists are marked with a dagger (†). For the convenience of readers I have included the address of the publisher in all possible cases. Where the entry first appeared in a magazine now discontinued, the name of the original publication is followed in parentheses by that of its successor, if any, as in Entry VIII below.

AUTHOR'S BIBLIOGRAPHY

†I. Canoeing Standards and Graded Classifications. American Camping Association, 343 S. Dearborn St., Chicago, Illinois.

*II. Report of the U. S. National Museum, 1899 (pages 523–537), by Otis T. Mason. U. S. National Museum, Washington.

III. "The Founding of Fort St. Joe," excerpt from Recollections, by Lieutenant Landman. *Sault Daily Star,* Sault Ste. Marie, Ont., Sept. 27, 1928.

*IV. "Canoes and Canoeing," by A. V. S. Pulling (Pierre Pulling). *Camper and Hiker,* April–August 1928.

*V. Souvenirs de Marine, by Captain Paris. (A French book, long out of print, available in some scientific libraries including the John Crerar Library, Chicago. The most important basic information on canoes and paddles known to the writer.)

†VI. Canoeing, by W. Van B. Claussen, with notes on Canoe History by John B. May. Merit Badge Library, Boy Scouts of America, 2 Park Ave., New York.

VII. "Notes on Canoeing," by A. V. S. Pulling (Pierre Pulling), with additional notes by John B. May. *Camps and Camping,* 1923.

VIII. "Strokes for Camp Canoeing," by A. V. S. Pulling (Pierre Pulling). *Camp Life,* December 1930 (*Camping Magazine,* 705 Park Ave., Plainfield, N. J.).

IX. "Canoe Nomenclature," ed. by Fred C. Mills and Howard Wakefield. *Camp Life,* December 1930 (*Camping Magazine,* 705 Park Ave., Plainfield, N. J.).

†X. HANDBOOK FOR CANOEING COUNSELORS, by Eleanor Deming. New City, N. Y.

XI. "The Camper Takes Stock of His Water Hazards," by Commodore W. E. Longfellow. *Camp Life,* April 1930 (*Camping Magazine,* 705 Park Ave., Plainfield, N. J.).

XII. "Woodcraft," by George R. Sears (Nessmuk). *Forest and Stream* (*Field & Stream,* 383 Madison Ave., New York.)

XIII. "War Canoeing," by A. V. S. Pulling (Pierre Pulling). *Camp Life,* May 1930 (*Camping Magazine,* 705 Park Ave., Plainfield, N. J.).

XIV. BOAT BUILDING, CANOE REPAIR, AND PADDLE MAKING, by Fred C. Mills. Service Library, Boy Scouts of America, 2 Park Ave., New York.

°XV. WITH GUN AND ROD IN CANADA (pages 141–174), by Phil H. Moore. Houghton Mifflin Co., 2 Park St., Boston.

XVI. "Bucking the Current," by Elon Jessup. *Field & Stream,* 383 Madison Ave., New York, May 1925.

XVII. CANOEING MANUAL 1952. New England Camping Association Inc., 14 Beacon St., Boston. (Written by an Association Committee of which Ann Elizabeth Weber was Chairman.)

†XVIII. THE CANOE: ITS SELECTION, CARE AND USE, by Robert Pinkerton. Macmillan Co., 60 Fifth Ave., New York.

°†XIX.   Boys' Book of Canoeing, by Elon Jessup. E. P.
Dutton & Co., Inc., 300 Fourth Ave., New York.

°XX.   "Paddle Drills," by Grace A. Thomas. *Camps and
Camping*, 1931.

°XXI.   Economic Woods, by Samuel J. Record. John
Wiley & Sons, Inc., 440 Fourth Ave., New York.

°†XXII.   The Elements of Canoeing, by A. V. S. Pulling (Pierre Pulling). Ann Arbor Press, Ann
Arbor, Mich.

BOY SCOUT BIBLIOGRAPHY

suggested in Boy Scouts' Merit Badge manual *Canoeing*.

†The Canoe: Its Selection, Care and Use, by Robert
Pinkerton (see XVIII above).

†The Canoe and You, by Ronald Perry. J. M. Dent &
Sons, Ltd., 25 Hollinger Rd., Toronto, Ont.

†Know Your Canoeing, by Morehouse and Fancher.
Western Division, American Canoe Association, 8224
So. Woodlawn Ave., Chicago.

How to Sail, by Samuel Carter III. Sentinel Book Pub-
lishers, Inc., 112 E. 19th St., New York.

MacKenzie and his Voyageurs, by Arthur P. Woolacott.
J. M. Dent & Sons, Ltd., 25 Hollinger Rd., Toronto,
Ont.

BIBLIOGRAPHY ON CANOEING AND BOATING

Suggested in the American Camping Association and the
New England Camping Association Canoeing Manual.

Boat Building and Canoe Repair. Boy Scout Publication No. 3145. Boy Scouts of America, 2 Park Ave.,
New York.

†Boys' Book of Canoeing, by Elon Jessup (see XIX above).

†Canoeing, by W. Van B. Claussen (see VI above).

Canoeing A to Z, by Ruth Elvedt. Burgess Publishing Co., 426 So. Sixth St., Minneapolis, Minn.

†Canoeing Standards and Graded Classification (see I above).

*†The Elements of Canoeing, by A. V. S. Pulling (see XXII above).

†Handbook for Canoeing Counselors, by Eleanor Deming (see X above).

†Know Your Canoeing, by Morehouse and Fancher (see Boy Scouts' list).

*Modern Camping Guide (chapter 4), by G. Martin. Appleton-Century-Crofts, Inc., 35 W. 32nd St., New York.

Official Aquatic Guides. Official Sports Library for Women, American Association for Health, Physical Education, and Recreation, 1201 16th St., N. W., Washington.

    Canoe Capers, by D. Horne. (Novelty events for programs of competition). 1943–44.

    Canoeing and Campcraft, by B. Hall. 1945–47.

    Canoeing Drills, by H. B. Lewis. (An eight-canoe drill for exhibition). 1943–44.

    Canoeing in Unprotected Waters, by W. Van B. Claussen. 1931–32.

    Canoeing Safety, by A. E. Weber. (Safety skills and stunts for the canoeing program). 1951–53.

    Canoeing Safety: Suggestions for Preliminary Tests, by M. Camp. 1935–36.

    Canoeing, by M. Camp. (Notes on selection, care, fundamental strokes, and safety). 1941.

    Development of Canoeing Standards, by M. Camp. 1931–32.

Safe Boat and Canoe Equipment for Camps, by
Commodore Longfellow. 1935–36.

Suggested Camp Program for Canoeing, by A. E.
Weber. 1947–49.

*Packing and Portaging, by Dillon Wallace. Outing
Handbooks, Macmillan Co., 60 Fifth Ave., New York.

The Boatman's Manual, by Carl Lane. W. W. Norton
& Co., Inc., 101 Fifth Ave., New York.

†The Canoe and You, by Ronald Perry (see Boy Scouts'
list).

†The Canoe: Its Selection, Care and Use, by Robert
Pinkerton (see XVIII above).

*Way of the Wilderness, by Calvin Rustrum. Burgess
Publishing Co., 426 So. Sixth St., Minneapolis, Minn.
(Excellent section on canoeing.)

Wildwood Wisdom (chapter 14), by Ellsworth Jaeger.
Macmillan Co., 60 Fifth Ave., New York.

UNITED STATES AND CANADIAN CANOE AND PADDLE MANUFACTURERS AND IMPORTERS

Aluma Craft Boat Co., 2633–27th Ave., Minneapolis 6,
Minn.

Bastien Bros., Loretteville, Quebec, Canada

Canadian Canoe Company Limited, Peterborough, Ont.,
Canada.

Chestnut Canoe Company Limited, Fredericton, N. B.,
Canada.

Folbot Corporation, Stark Industrial Park, Charleston,
S. C.

Grumman Aircraft Engineering Corporation, Bethpage,
Long Island, N. Y.

Joys Bros. Co., 129 No. Water St., Milwaukee 2, Wis.

Kayak Boat Company, 152 E. 129th St., New York, N. Y.

Kennebec Canoe Company, Waterville, Me.

Klepper Company, 1472 Broadway, New York, N. Y.

Link Aviation Devices, Binghamton, N. Y.

Montague Oar and Paddle Company, Foxboro, Mass.

New York Boat and Oar Company, 40 Rector St., New York, N. Y.

Old Town Canoe Company, Old Town, Me.

Penn Yan Boats, Inc., Penn Yan, N. Y.

Peterborough Canoe Company Limited, Peterborough, Ont., Canada

Rhinelander Boat and Canoe Company, Rhinelander, Wis.

Seminole Canoe Company, Fort Myers, Fla.

Skowhegan Boat and Canoe Company, Norridgewock, Me.

C. W. Stiver, Saginaw, Mich.

St. Louis Boat and Motor Company, 720 N. Commercial St., St. Louis, Mo.

Thompson Bros. Boat Mfg. Company, Cortland, N. Y.

Thompson Bros. Boat Mfg. Company, Peshtigo, Wis.

E. M. White Canoe Company, Old Town, Me.

Willits Brothers Canoe Company, 2404 Day Island Blvd., Tacoma, Wash.

Index

Boldface numerals indicate page on which illustration is located.